FEMINISM À LA QUÉBÉCOISE

FEMINISM À LA QUÉBÉCOISE

MICHELINE DUMONT

Translated by Nicole Kennedy

Feminist History Society / Société d'histoire féministe

Ottawa

ISBN
978-0-9866478-2-6

TRANSLATED BY
Nicole Kennedy

EDITED BY
Sarah Swartz

DESIGN
Zab Design & Typography Inc.

*The National Assembly of Québec
before 1968 was referred to as Assemblée
Législative or Parlement Provincial. We
haved used National Assembly throughout.*

*We have used French place names unless
they are part of the English title for an
organization.*

Feminist History Society is a project of
the Women's Education and Research
Foundation of Ontario Inc.

BECOME A MEMBER
www.FeministHistories.ca

La Société d'histoire féministe est un
projet de la Women's Education and
Research Foundation of Ontario Inc.

DEVENEZ MEMBRE
www.FeministHistories.ca

To my granddaughter Camille, my first reader,
born a century after the founding of the National Council
of Women of Canada in 1893

CONTENTS

FEMINIST HISTORY SOCIETY

The Feminist History Society is committed to creating a lasting record of the women's movement in Canada and Québec for the period between 1960 and the year of the Society's founding, 2010. Our objective is to celebrate fifty years of activity and accomplishment by creating a written legacy, for ourselves, our families and friends, our communities, students, and scholars. The beautiful books we publish, with membership support, will be as spirited and diverse as the movement itself, meant to stand together, and to encourage and challenge those who follow.

Invoking the image of a wave on water—of a visible, moving, growing rise of energy—many have described the feminist campaigns for suffrage and temperance during the nineteenth and early twentieth centuries as the "first wave of feminism." Thus the upsurge of feminist activism that began in the 1960s has often been characterized as the "second wave." The concept of "waves" with respect to the history of the women's movement is debated. Feminism has a history that predates the 1960s and will continue long after 2010. The energy that women brought to their quest for equality in these decades, however, is beyond dispute, and it is that energy that we seek to capture in this series.

In 1960, the Voice of Women was founded. The decade of the 1960s also saw the founding of the Fédération des femmes du Québec, the appointment of the Royal Commission on the Status of Women, and the creation of "women's liberation" groups across the country. By 2010, as some of the founding mothers of our generation of feminism have begun to die, it serves as a wake-up call regarding the pressing need to chronicle our history. Our movement is not at an end. But new waves are upon us, and now is the time to take stock of what we did and how we did it.

Over the next decade, our goal is to publish two or three books a year chronicling different aspects of the movement from sea to sea to sea. Members of the non-profit Feminist History Society receive an annual book at no extra charge, and may also purchase other books published by the Society. The topics will be as diverse as our wide-ranging campaigns for equality through transformative social, economic, civil, political, and cultural change. We will make every effort to be inclusive of race, class, geography, culture, dis/ability, language, sexual identity, and age.

We maintain an open call for submissions. There will be many different authors, as individuals and organizations who participated in the movement are encouraged to contribute. There will be a variety of formats, including autobiographies, biographies, single- and multi-themed volumes, edited collections, pictorial histories, plays, and novels.

Beth Atcheson, Constance Backhouse, Lorraine Greaves, Diana Majury and Beth Symes form the working collective for the Society. Shari Graydon has shared her expertise and time to help move the Society forward. Mary Breen, Miranda Edwards, and Jane Will have helped with the Society's administration. Martin Dufresne is providing expert translation services. Dawn Buie has created the Society's web site, making it simple to join and contact us. Zab of Zab Design & Typography has created the distinctive visual identity for the Society, as well as the book design for the series. We offer our heartfelt thanks to all of the talented and committed feminists who are providing encouragement, advice, and support.

We wish to especially acknowledge the contribution of those who have made it possible to publish *Feminism à la Québécoise*. Les éditions du remue-ménage embraced the idea from the beginning, and generously granted permission for this edition to proceed. Micheline Dumont has worked closely, over months, with translator Nicole Kennedy and English editor Sarah Swartz to retain the integrity and character of the original French text for English-speaking readers. It is a privilege for us to publish this book, and we express our deep gratitude to Micheline, Nicole and Sarah for their commitment to this effort.

We urge you to join, and to participate as an author, in the Feminist History Society.

www.FeministHistories.ca | info@FeministHistories.ca

LA SOCIÉTÉ D'HISTOIRE FÉMINISTE

La Société d'histoire féministe s'est donné pour mandat de créer un portrait durable du mouvement des femmes au Canada et au Québec entre les années 1960 et 2010, l'année de fondation de la Société. Nous voulons ainsi célébrer cinquante ans d'activité et de réussites en créant un legs imprimé pour nous-mêmes, nos familles et nos proches, nos communautés et nos élèves, ainsi que pour faciliter la recherche. Les superbes livres que nous publions, grâce au soutien de nos membres, seront aussi vivants et diversifiés que le mouvement lui-même, et nous espérons que leur combinaison encouragera et provoquera celles qui nous suivront dans cette voie.

Invoquant l'image d'une vague avançant sur l'eau—symbole d'une montée graduelle d'énergie visible et mobile—beaucoup ont décrit les campagnes féministes organisées pour revendiquer le droit de vote et la tempérance, au dix-neuvième et au début du vingtième siècle, comme la « première vague du féminisme .» Ainsi, la poussée d'activisme féministe qui a débuté dans les années 1960 a souvent été caractérisée comme une « deuxième vague .» Toutefois, cette notion de « vagues » ne fait pas consensus comme modèle de l'histoire du mouvement des femmes. Il est certain que le féminisme date d'avant les années 1960 et se poursuivra bien au-delà de 2010. Mais on ne peut mettre en doute l'incroyable dynamisme des femmes dans leur quête d'égalité au cours des cinq dernières décennies; c'est cette énergie que nous voulons illustrer avec notre collection.

L'année 1960 a été celle de la fondation du groupe La Voix des femmes. Cette décennie a aussi vu la fondation de la Fédération des femmes du Québec, la mise sur pied de la Commission royale d'enquête sur la condition de la femme au Canada et l'apparition de groupes de « libération des femmes » partout au pays. Cinquante ans plus tard, le décès de quelques-unes des pionnières de ce mouvement sonne le rappel d'un besoin pressant, celui de rédiger la chronique de notre histoire. Ce n'est aucunement la fin du mouvement. Mais de nouvelles mouvances nous sollicitent, et il est temps de faire le point sur ce que nous avons accompli et comment nous y sommes arrivées.

Au cours des prochains dix ans, notre objectif est de publier deux ou trois livres par an, qui relateront différents aspects du mouvement féministe dans toutes les régions du pays. Les membres de notre société sans but lucratif reçoivent gratuitement un livre par an et peuvent aussi acheter les autres livres publiés par la Société. Nos thèmes seront aussi diversifiés que nos grandes campagnes pour l'égalité et leurs réformes sociales, économiques, civiles, politiques et culturelles. Nous nous efforcerons d'être inclusives à tous les titres : origine ethnique, classe, géographie, culture, (in)capacité, langue, identité sexuelle et âge.

Nous maintenons une invitation générale à nous soumettre des manuscrits, en y encourageant toutes les personnes et organisations ayant participé au mouvement. Cette diversité de plumes pourra exploiter une foule de genres, qu'il s'agisse de biographies, d'auto-biographies, d'ouvrages à un ou plusieurs thèmes, d'anthologies, de récits en images, de pièces ou de romans.

Beth Atcheson, Constance Backhouse, Lorraine Greaves, Diana Majury et Beth Symes forment la collective de travail de la Société. Shari Graydon contribue à notre avancement en nous faisant bénéficier de son expertise et de son temps. Mary Breen, Miranda Edwards et Jane Will nous ont aidées à mettre en place la procédure administrative. Martin Dufresne s'acquitte de services experts en traduction. Dawn Buie a mis en ligne le site Web de la Société, qui facilite les adhésions et nos contacts avec le public. Zab, de Zab Design & Typography, a créé notre identité visuelle distinctive et une maquette de livres pour notre collection. Et nous adressons nos remerciements les plus sincères aux féministes talentueuses et engagées qui nous assurent sans relâche encouragements, conseils et soutien.

Nous souhaitons reconnaître particulièrement la contribution des femmes qui ont rendu possible la publication de Feminism à la Québécoise. Les éditions du remue-ménage ont embrassé l'idée dès la toute première heure et ont généreusement autorisé ce processus d'édition. Micheline Dumont a collaboré étroitement, durant plusieurs mois, avec la traductrice Nicole Kennedy et la relectrice Sarah Swartz afin de préserver l'intégrité et le caractère du texte français de départ au profit de notre auditoire anglophone. C'est pour nous un privilège de publier cet ouvrage et nous sommes très reconnaissantes à Micheline, Nicole et Sarah pour le dévouement qu'elles ont consacré à ce projet.

Quant à vous, nous vous incitons ardemment à vous joindre à la Société d'histoire féministe et à y participer à titre d'auteure.

www.FeministHistories.ca | info@FeministHistories.ca

PREFACE

WE ARE VERY PROUD to present the third volume in our Feminist History Society series. Our first volume was Marguerite Andersen's *Feminist Journeys/Voies féministes,* an historical tribute to feminist awakening in Canada told through the voices of ninety-four women who describe what inspired them to identify as second wave feminists. *Feminist Journeys* was followed by *Writing the Revolution* in which Michele Landsberg offered a window into the second wave movement through the eyes of a prize-winning feminist journalist whose columns chronicled on-the-ground issues and events. Our third volume is the first of our series to focus on a specific region, delving into the remarkable women and fascinating activities that shaped the feminist movement in Québec.

Micheline Dumont is an illustrious Québec women's historian. Her brilliant *Le féminisme québécois raconté à Camille,* published in French in 2008 by the Montréal feminist publishing house Les éditions du remue-ménage, quickly became a Québec best-seller. Now translated for the Feminist History Society by Nicole Kennedy, this volume is the first opportunity non French-speaking feminists will have to learn about the distinctive paths feminism took in Québec.

Although Québec shared the energy and vibrancy of the second wave women's movement with the other regions of Canada, its history was unique. Distinct from English Canada in terms of language, culture, religion, politics, economics, and law, Québec feminism often took its own route. Not surprisingly, the Québec story takes new turns and directions, with narratives peopled with a roster of names and landmark events as yet largely unheralded in English Canada. And as noted by its first women's historians, the Clio Collective, chronology of Québec feminism had a timeline all its own.

Unlike our other books in this series, which focus on the decades between 1960 and 2010, to tell the tale of Québec feminism requires a longer sweep, stretching back into the late 19th century for an explanation of the late arrival of women's right to vote, access to public education, and integration into the paid workplace. Micheline Dumont starts her recounting of Québec feminism beginning in 1893 with the establishment of the French wing of the National Council of Women of Canada/Conseil national des femmes du Canada. She follows Québec feminists through their protracted struggles for suffrage and other legal change, through the Quiet Revolution of the 1960s, and into the upsurge of the feminist movement that took Québec by storm in the ensuing decades.

Although they shared many ideas and objectives, feminists in other regions of Canada rarely knew what their sister activists in Québec were up to. The linguistic divide created the same "two solitudes" that afflicted much of the rest of the country. It was a tragic gap, which left English Canadian feminists ignorant of the innovative strategies pursued by their Québec sisters, unaware of the exciting and disparate directions honed by the movement in Québec. It was a chasm that would frequently bedevil efforts to establish national or pan-Canadian feminist campaigns and organizations, as later books in this series will demonstrate.

The time has come to share the story of the exploits of the daring Québécoises, who drew their influences from France, from the United States, and only partially from English Canada. The world they aspired to was in direct opposition to the ties that bound them to second-class citizenship in the 19th century, and deeply immersed in the Québec independence movement at large. Micheline Dumont's book is a tribute to the originality and creativity of Québec feminism. It is must reading for Canadian feminists.

FOREWORD

I WROTE THIS BOOK for young women—like my granddaughter, Camille—who were born at the end of the 20th century to tell them the story of feminism in Québec from 1893 to the present. I also wrote for readers who are put off by scholarly books and research reports bristling with footnotes. Though it's an easy read, all the information in this book is backed up by studies, thesis papers, monographs, and other documents. To make it more accessible, I have placed all references for the quotations at the end of the book.

This volume is a translation of *Le féminisme québécois raconté à Camille*, published in 2008 by the feminist publishing house in Montréal, Les éditions du remue-ménage. Since the chronology of Québec feminism has rarely been aligned with that of the English Canadian feminist movement, this book provides a good opportunity for the pan-Canadian public to become aware of this distinct component of French Canadian feminism and its history. I hope this story will be inspiring to Canadian feminists and will convince all readers that feminism is very much alive.

— MICHELINE DUMONT, *July 2012*

FEMINISM À LA QUÉBÉCOISE

PROLOGUE

Young Women in 1890

THE YEAR IS 1890. Ernestine, Berthe, Marie, Antoinette, Eugénie, and Imelda are 17 years old. Almost all of them have been to school. Like all good French Canadian girls, they say their catechism and prayers every day. They far surpass their brothers in their knowledge of reading, writing, and arithmetic. Some of them went to Catholic boarding schools, where they learned English, music, literature, and history. But higher education is out of the question: no colleges or vocational schools for them. University is prohibited, unless of course, they are Anglophone, rich, and Protestant.

At the end of the 19th century, young women were not free to read or write whatever they liked; their actions were closely monitored. The list of things they were forbidden to do was much longer than the list of things they were allowed to do. A girl's reputation or "virtue" was much more important than that of a boy. Brides had to be virgins when they got married, while young bridegrooms were supposed to be sexually experienced. The double standard was very much alive and well.

Early marriage was the goal, but for large numbers of women this was not to be. Young women who had not married by the age of 25 were considered "spinsters." And the employment options for women were limited.

If they had earned their "model diploma" (equivalent of grade 10), young women could teach, usually in a rural school. They were paid much less than male teachers. Young women who lived in the country worked in the family home and on the farm. There was much work to be done, so all the children pitched in.

Many young women left for the city, where it was easier to find work, as servants in the homes of the rich for example. Jobs were also available in factories, stores, and offices. In the cities, most working class girls did not finish school. Those who remained in school longer, until they were 14 or 15, might get work in an office or a store. When mothers worked outside the home, the eldest daughter was expected to look after her younger siblings.

The pay for young women was extremely low. As soon as a woman got married, her employer let her go. Should women even have the right to work was a popular topic of discussion. Most people believed that paid work should be left to the men. In cities and the countryside, the longer girls stayed in school, the less they were expected to work. For those who could afford it, school was to keep young women busy until they got married. People believed that to work for a living was not "womanly"—many even considered it disreputable. But there was never a problem with women doing all the cooking, cleaning, washing, ironing, and household chores.

If they married, women were expected to have lots of children. They were forced to take their husbands' names, for example, Mrs. Édouard Lanctôt or Mrs. George Desforges. Under the *Civil Code of Québec*, Québec's laws governing marriage and other aspects of life, women were considered incompetent. Treated as unable to care for themselves, like children and persons with mental disabilities, married women had to ask their husbands to sign for them. If a married woman was allowed to continue in paid work, her salary belonged to her husband. If her husband died, the mother could not become the legal guardian of her own children. If the couple had separated (which was rare at that time), their children stayed with the father. This was the law. When it came to inheritance, boys were almost always given preference. It was unfair, but it was considered improper to protest or even mention these inequities. Girls were taught to accept their lot.

Their grandmothers, in the early 19th century, had been entitled to vote. But, in 1834, male politicians decided that this practice was unacceptable, even offensive. In the name of public interest, decency, and modesty, women were no longer allowed to enter a

Blanche Castonguay (1886-1967) the grandmother of the author, at age 16 in the early 1900s. Black stockings, high collar, long sleeves: a dress code that eloquently illustrates the social control of women.

polling station. In 1867, at the time of Confederation, men drafting the constitution made sure that, under the law, only men would be considered "persons." Men ruled the public sphere, controlling politics, elections, business, contracts, school boards, parishes, and the railroads. It was women's responsibility to take care of the family, the children, and, in some cases, to take care of others through charitable work.

Women had so few options that many girls decided to enter the convent. After a few years in a Catholic boarding school, many young women experienced the "calling." This was an easy choice because people in Québec society were deeply religious. Once she had become a nun, a woman could teach, study, care for the sick and work in charitable institutions like hospices, orphanages, mental asylums, and shelters. Nuns took care of people with disabilities such as blindness and deafness, juvenile delinquents, women prisoners, and unwed mothers. They even travelled on missions to South America, the Yukon, or Western Canada, regions still relatively unexplored. The religious calling became increasingly popular among young women. Some nuns had important responsibilities in their convents, with titles like General Superior, *Économe générale* [Treasurer], and *Directrice générale des études*, representing all the teaching orders and generally responsible for teacher training, curricula, textbooks, examinations, and relations with government and religious authorities.

In the cities, people witnessed the emergence of inventions like the railroads, the telephone, and gas and electric lighting. Newspapers were full of stories of women's achievements in other countries, where women were becoming doctors, lawyers, biologists, journalists, and opera singers. In the United States, universities were accepting female students. There was a sense that new horizons were beginning to open for women. The "new woman" was a popular topic of conversation among the upper class and intelligentsia. Young women of that era felt very "modern." They were moving into the 20th century.

Industrialization had also ushered in a new social class: the middle class or *petite bourgeoisie*. Women of this class employed servants and could live a life of leisure. But many of these women wanted something more than the card parties, teas and balls of high society. They threw themselves into charitable work: hospitals, orphanages, and soup kitchens. Women who supported charitable institutions through various fundraising activities were known as "society matrons." They held fundraising events, visited the sick, and did volunteer work. This was called philanthropy. Young middle class girls were recruited to do this work as soon as they left boarding school.

Most young women thus found themselves in a very narrow, protected, and tightly monitored world. Like their mothers, they did not question their situation. Except, that is, for a few more informed and daring women: the feminists.

Who were these feminists? And what exactly was meant by feminism in 1890?

La P[atrie]

29e ANNEE—No 77 DOUZE PAGES MONTREA[L]

LA FEDERATION NATIONALE DES

Intéressantes choses dites à la séance
l'Association. —

La séance d'ouverture du premier congrès annuel de la Fédération Nationale des femmes canadiennes-françaises a été véritablement ce qu'elle avait promis d'être, à savoir un événement social, artistique et littéraire.

La présence à cette soirée d'ouverture de Son Excellence Sir Louis Jetté, ainsi que d'un public aussi distingué que nombreux donnait à cette réunion un caractère très brillant. Pour ne citer que quelques noms, disons que Mgr l'archevêque, assistait avec son conjuteur Mgr Racicot, puis venaient ensuite l'hon. Rodolphe Lemieux et Mme Lemieux, l'hon. sénateur Béique et Mme Béique, Sir Alex. Lacoste et Lady Lacoste, l'hon. juge Saint-Pierre et Mme Saint-Pierre, l'hon. sénateur L. O. David et Mme David, le docteur Rottot, l'hon. sénateur Dandurand et Mme Dandurand, l'échevin DeSerres et Mme DeSerres, le chanoine Roy, le chanoine Gauthier, M. l'abbé E. Auclair, le R. P. Louis Lalande, M. et Mme C. Martin, M. J. J. Beauchamp, M. J. C. Beauchamp, M. Art. Gagnon, Mme Gérin-Lajoie, Mlle Saint-Jean, Mme Huguenin, Mlles M. Beaupré, A. M. Vaillant, Mme Ph. Roy, Mme Globensky, Mme A. Gagnon, Mme Hone Hudon, Mlle Cartier, Mlle Labelle, Mlle Bienvenue, Mlle de Beaujeu, Mlle Anctil, Mlle Lajoie, Mme H. Pelletier, Mme L. D. Mignault, Mme P. B. Mignault, Mme L. Rodier, Mme J. Tessier, Mlle Renault, Mme Rottot, Dr Irma Levasseur, Mme Provencher, Mme E. Bouthillier, Mme Mathys, Mlle A. Lanctôt (Camille), Mlle Nantel, Mlle Lesage (Colette), Mlle Charbonneau, Mme Leman, Mlle Marceau, Mlle Frappier, Mlle Viger, Mme Cocher,

LADY JETTE, présidente d'honneur aux séances de la Fédération.

Mlle Auclair, Mme Côté, Mlle Gervais, Mlles Longtin, Meunier, Mme Henry Hamilton, Mme J. R. Thibaudeau, Mlle Victoria Cartier, Mlle Laurin, Mlle Bibeau, Mlles Lalime, Labelle, Samson, Généreux, Pelletier, Bourbonnière, Mayrand, Bélanger, Lalime, Valois, Godbout, Rivard, M. A. St-Pierre.

Un événement artistique, la soirée d'hier le fut par le concours précieux de Mme H. C. Saint-Pierre, de Mlle Idola Saint-Jean, de Mme Damien Masson, de Mme Hone Hudon, de Mlle L. Bienvenu et de M. Toranto.

CONCERT D'OUVERTURE

L'ouverture au piano exécutée par Mme Saint-Pierre, a obtenu le succès le plus complet, et a vite mis de l'entrain dans l'auditoire. Mlle Saint-Jean s'est conquise hier soir d'autres et de nombreux admirateurs, et les applaudissements qui l'ont accueillis, comme ceux qui l'ont acclamée après sa récitation de "les deux

Mme BEIQUE, présidente de la Fédération.

SIR LOUIS [...]

parole à la [...]

noces" de Per[...]
preuve que [...]
art une adm[...]
monologue a[...]
de Jules C[...]
Masson avec [...]
été les inte[...]
Mme Hone-[...]
thique avec [...]
du sur le vi[...]
le mot n'est [...]
et "Sérénade"[...]
coutumier a[...]
se" de Saras[...]

UN SQUELETTE DANS
LES BROUSSAILLES

UN DRAME AU

Patrie

Une Chambre Vide

C'est une chose qui ne devr
exister pour qui lit les color
demandes de " LaPatrie".

Comment la Louer

1 | WOMEN ORGANIZE
1893-1912

NDI, 27   N CENTIN

MMES CANADIENNES-FRANÇAISES

uverture du premier Congrès annuel de
Quatre discours

bay. Tous ces artistes ont eu les ac-
clamations que leur talent d'exécution
a provoqué chez l'auditoire de
choix qui les exécutait.

LA PORTÉE LITTÉRAIRE

de cette séance d'ouverture se réduit
à quatre allocutions seulement, mais
hâtons nous de dire que la forme de
ces pièces littéraires, leur richesse de
styles et d'idées, ainsi que leur débit
n'ont pas peu contribué à donner à
la soirée un cachet particulier.

Ainsi, Mme Béïque, dans son allo-
cution de bienvenue a bien su faire
ressortir la solennité de la circons-

qui a adressé la
d'hier.

et, lui sont une
pour elle et son
ncère. La ré-
noces", est un
ation musicale
e Mme Damiea
e Toranto ont
e Granier. Puis
oujours sympa-
on admirable-
rop—"Tristesse
ard. Enfin, M.
tria dont il est
Danse hongroi-
phir" de Hu-

Mme GÉRIN-LAJOIE, fondatrice
de la Fédération.

Sa Grandeur Mgr BRUCHÉSI, qui a
adressé la parole à la séance d'hier

tance qui réunissait pour la première
fois nos jeunes Canadiennes françaises pour affirmer

LEUR RÔLE SOCIAL.

L'association Saint-Jean Baptiste,
dit-elle, va désormais devenir le lieu
de réunion des femmes canadiennes-
françaises. On pourra peut-être se
demander si ce n'est pas là du féminisme ?

Je réponds oui sans hésiter, mais
je me hâte d'ajouter qu'il y a deux
sortes de féminisme. Le féminisme ré-
volutionnaire qui a pour but d'éloi-

gner la femme de son rôle et de son
foyer, et le féminisme chrétien qui a
pour but l'amour du prochain et du
devoir. Nous ne voulons pas mériter
le reproche que l'on fait à la femme
de sortir de sa sphère. Aussi notre
première affirmation a-t-elle été la
création d'une école ménagère, où
l'on apprend un art essentiellement
domestique. L'éducation dans les
couvents s'est tournée dans cette direction et l'on forme aujourd'hui des
femmes d'intérieur et des mères. Or,
la charité, et le dévouement n'ap-
partiennent-ils pas aux femmes d'intérieur et aux mères? Il importe
donc pour les femmes de faire des
études sur les conditions sociales, de
s'enquérir du bien que l'on fait ail-
leurs pour en trouver une application profitable ici. La Fédération
est le moyen de faciliter ces études,
et elle répond à un besoin en opé-
rant le bien, partout où elle se
trouve.

L'ÉGLISE ET LES FÉDÉRATION
FÉMINISTES

Du reste l'Église, elle-même, ap-
prouve ces fédérations. Au dernier
congrès de Boulogne, il y a quelques années, l'Église elle-même ne
déclara-t-elle pas qu'il était urgent
que toutes les énergies féminines s'u-
nissant, pour que les femmes com-
battirent la révolution par l'ardeur
de leur foi. Au Canada, la religion
n'est pas menacée, mais il n'en reste
pas moins un champ très vaste à
couvrir. Mgr Bruchési lui-même a
suggéré les champs d'action où le
zèle de la femme peut le mieux s'af-

(Suite à la 8e page)

LIEU DU FLEUVE UNE CÉRÉMONIE
IMPRESSIONNANTE

CHAPTER I

Feminist Beginnings

La Patrie,
see p. 30

IN THE LATE 19TH CENTURY, in many countries women met together in political associations to discuss their rights. The oldest of these associations was formed at the Seneca Falls Women's Rights Convention, New York State, in 1848. They sprang up in nearly every country in Europe, the Americas, and even as far as Asia and North Africa. These groups existed even before the words "feminism" and "feminist." At the time, people referred to "the rights of woman." The condition of women in many countries resembled that of women in Québec in the mid 19th century. There were no "feminist" groups in Québec; no one even knew the word existed. The word "feminism" in French originally referred to a rare disease described in medical dictionaries. A man with female physical traits (no beard, prominent breasts) was said to suffer from "féminisme."

Around 1870, women's rights activists in France were very outspoken, to the chagrin of many men. These women were ridiculed by a leading French writer, son of the celebrated author Alexandre Dumas. He called them *féministes*, insinuating they wanted to be men and adopt male characteristics. Ten years later, Hubertine Auclert, a French activist, thought this word perfectly described the struggle for women's rights and declared herself a *féministe*. The term *féminisme* quickly followed. Since the word translated easily into many languages, it immediately caught on throughout Europe and was used in reference to groups that protested women's inferior status in society and made demands for women's rights. The 1890s was the decade of the first international feminist conventions.

What did these feminists want? Their list of demands was long. Essentially, they declared that women's inferior status was not "natural," but rather socially and culturally imposed on women.

They wanted to change the laws, regulations, and traditions that were responsible for what they called the subordination of women. Feminists revolted against this subordination and demanded change on many fronts: especially education, employment, and the law.

Numerous women wanted to continue their education beyond the elementary or secondary level, and even to attend university. The right to education was considered to be the foundation of all other rights, for three reasons: education develops the consciousness of one's rights; education reinforces self-confidence; and education paves the way to economic independence. These reasons were borne out in women's aspirations and actions. Once they had completed their schooling, growing numbers of women were eager to obtain paid employment.

Many women became journalists and defended their ideas in the newspapers. The right to paid employment was central to feminist demands. They demanded higher pay and better working conditions, shorter work days and a healthier work environment. Women working in the same jobs as men demanded equal pay. Feminists called for the hiring of female inspectors in factories employing women. In Québec, feminists wanted women to have the right to become doctors, lawyers, pharmacists, accountants, and architects—just like American women.

Feminists in Québec also wanted to amend the *Civil Code of Québec*, which defined women as legally incompetent and their husbands' dependants. They wanted to eliminate the inequalities and double standards enshrined in the *Code*. Reforms of the laws governing marriage and the family were a major component of women activists' demands. Married women had to take their husband's name and could do nothing legal without his signature. At the end of the 19th century, according to the law, children belonged to the father, and, when a couple separated, custody of the children went to him. Moreover, feminists protested the fact that while women's sexuality was highly suspect, the sexual conduct of men was always beyond reproach. This was called the double standard. They demanded better protection for married women and the right to maintain custody of their children. Feminists also wanted to raise the legal age for marriage, which, at the time, was 12 for girls and 14 for boys. The more daring among them even demanded the right to initiate divorce, which was already effective in countries like France and the United States. Reforms of civil laws governing marriage and the family were a major component of women activists' demands.

Many feminists focused on suffrage (the right to vote) and civil rights, so that women could be full-fledged citizens. Yet, this demand of full citizenship was not accepted by all feminists; some believed it was much too extreme. When people began campaigning for universal suffrage in the mid-19th century, this so-called "universal right" was held exclusively by a limited class of men. To challenge this privileged male stronghold was a daunting task. However, if at first not all feminists considered the right to vote a priority, by the turn of the 20th century, it had become one.

Many feminists focused their attention on local issues and pressing social problems. Feminists were very active at the municipal level. They called for green spaces in the cities, healthier living conditions in working class neighbourhoods, public bathhouses, and kindergartens. A century ago, feminists devoted a lot of attention to criminal law issues such as alcoholism, prostitution (then called the "white slave trade"), and obscene literature. They realized that poverty was usually the reason women ended up in prostitution, and understood the particular vulnerability of female servants. Feminists were also concerned about the poor living conditions of female prisoners and in girls' reform schools.

Many women campaigned with temperance associations, formed to advocate for the prohibition of the sale of alcohol. Alcohol abuse was viewed as the enemy of the family. Prohibition was one of the main reasons why women wanted the vote: These women wanted the power to change the laws governing the sale of alcohol.

A few daring women even discussed birth control—a truly remarkable step for that time. Not only were birth control and abortion punishable as crimes under the *Criminal Code*, but even discussion of these subjects in public was strictly forbidden. Condemned by all the churches, these topics were not even discussed within most feminists associations. But Québec feminists did not advocate for sexual freedom. They feared being associated with the few women in France and in the United States who defended women's sexual freedom and led "free" sexual lives. They believed that such women discredited the feminist movement.

Feminists criticized the dress code that was imposed on women, because it restricted their movement. They wanted to play sports and ride bicycles without being denounced.

Last, feminists believed that women merited social protection. Social rights were undeveloped in the early 1900s; governments had not yet set up programs for the unemployed, the poor, the sick, and the elderly. It was generally accepted that all such problems should be addressed by charity alone. Feminists challenged the charity model. They demanded pensions for poor women and women who had been abandoned by their husbands. They pressed to obtain services for mothers, medical assistance for childbirth, and children's hospitals.

Feminists were realistic and practical minded. Some of their demands had already been met in other countries. By 1890, for example, thousands of women in the United States were attending university and had careers as doctors and lawyers. In New Zealand, women had won the vote in 1893. In English Canada, groups had been fighting for women's rights since the 1850s and the legal status of wives had been amended in Ontario in 1872.

Québec had yet to see the emergence of any specifically feminist activist groups. Middle class women were busy with their charities. They heard vague murmurings of feminist progress in the United States, Great Britain, and France, but only a very few wealthy women and journalists really knew what was happening.

What would ignite the flame of feminist activism in Québec?

CHAPTER 2

Women in Montréal and the National Council of Women of Canada

AS THE 19ᵀᴴ CENTURY drew to a close, women in Canada, like their sisters in Europe and the United States, were coming together in organizations with a broad range of goals, including temperance societies campaigning against the sale of alcohol, society matrons' organizations doing philanthropic work, literary societies, study circles, alumnae clubs (female graduates from institutions of higher education), professional associations, Masonic lodges, religious and missionary groups, and even, in Toronto, a small group dedicated to gaining the right for women to vote.

In 1888, a strong movement emerged from a number of countries with the aim of creating a single international organization to unite women activists around the world. That year, a group of women representing seven countries created the International Council of Women in Washington, D.C. May Wright Sewall, a women's suffrage activist from the United States, toured Europe to promote the creation of national councils in every country. Five years later, in 1893, delegates from 35 countries met in Chicago where they elected their first president, Lady Ishbel Aberdeen, an English aristocrat. The delegates chose a woman from the elite upper class to show that they were not "common" revolutionaries and to distance themselves from more radical groups which were organizing in several countries during this period.

Lord Aberdeen was named Governor General of Canada in 1893. His wife, Lady Aberdeen, immediately created an association so that Canadian women could participate in the Council's meeting in Chicago. In 1893, she helped women form a broad coalition, uniting all of the women's groups in Canada. This was the birth of the National Council of Women of Canada/Conseil national

des femmes du Canada. It was, and remains, a non-partisan organization, open to women of different religions and to both English and French Canadians in order to create a stronger vehicle with which to defend women's rights. The first members believed that women's "naturally" generous and compassionate natures would transform society and heal the social ills caused by the industrial revolution taking place in the cities: slums, poverty, infant mortality, epidemics, alcoholism, prostitution, children born out of wedlock. Women demanded equality with men. While this position was far from unanimous, women continued to debate and seek the best way of exerting pressure on governments.

Ishbel, Marchioness of Aberdeen and Temair (1857-1939), better known as Lady Aberdeen, was the first president of the International Council of Women. Pictured here in 1893, when her husband was appointed Governor General of Canada, she founded the National Council of Women of Canada/Conseil national des femmes du Canada.

The National Council of Women of Canada organized regular conventions in the country's largest cities to hear what was on women's minds with the goal of eventually passing on their demands to the different levels of government. Members learned how to draft motions, gather signatures for petitions, propose amendments to draft legislation, monitor political debates, and argue their ideas

LE MONDE ILLUSTRÉ

| 1ère année, No. 4.—Samedi, 31 mai 1884. Bureaux : 25, rue Saint-Gabriel, Montréal. | LE No. 5 CENTS. | ABONNEMENTS : Six mois : $1.50. — Un an : $3.00. |

Imprimé par la Cie Lithographique Burland.

MADAME HON. J. R. THIBAUDEAU,

Présidente de la Kermesse.

in the newspapers. Women in several cities set up Local Councils in order to coordinate their groups' activities.

Marguerite Lamothe-Thibaudeau (1853-1939) was one of the founders of Notre-Dame Hospital, a member of the Montreal Local Council of Women, and an active philanthropist. She presided over the Francophone section of the Red Cross during World War I.

In 1893, the same year that the National Council was born, three Local Councils opened in Canada: in Toronto, Hamilton, and Montréal. In 1894, 11 others were formed, including one in Québec City. A movement had truly emerged. The popularity of the National Council of Women of Canada was now undeniable and it kept growing. In 1895 women established six new councils. The leaders of these Local Councils were all English-speaking Protestant women. This represented a major obstacle to the participation of French Canadian women. Indeed, religious authorities in Montréal banned Catholic groups from joining the new organization. Lady Aberdeen made a personal appeal for support to Monsignor Fabre, Archbishop of the Diocese of Montréal, but was unable to sway him. He would only allow individual women to join, and they could be counted on one hand. But those who did join were leaders: three of these women became central figures in the budding women's movement in Québec.

First, there was Marguerite Lamothe-Thibaudeau. A former beauty queen, she surprised everyone in 1881, a year after the founding of Notre-Dame Hospital, when she became the director of an association of society matrons affiliated with the hospital, Dames patronnesses de l'hôpital Notre-Dame. At that time, society matrons played a major role in the funding of hospitals, and Montrealers considered Madame Thibaudeau one of the hospital's founders. In 1893, during the National Council's first year of operation, Marguerite Lamothe-Thibaudeau was appointed to the position of vice-president of the Montreal Local Council of Women (Conseil local des femmes de Montréal). Though she shied away from the limelight, she nevertheless wielded enormous influence. She was the one who organized conferences, reserved rooms for meetings, obtained permissions from the Archbishop, and handled public relations. Public speaking terrified her, however, and the following year she was replaced at the Council by Joséphine Marchand-Dandurand, one of the most high profile women among Québec's political elite.

Joséphine Marchand-Dandurand (1861-1925) was the editor of one of the first women's magazines, *Le Coin du feu*, from 1893 to 1896, and a member of the Executive Committee of the National Council of Women of Canada. She and her husband, Raoul Dandurand, were members of the Canadian government delegation to the International Exhibition of Paris in 1900.

Joséphine Marchand-Dandurand was a journalist from a famous Liberal family. In 1893, she realized a longstanding dream when she created her own magazine, *Le Coin du feu*. Almost single-handedly, she edited and wrote for the magazine, occasionally inviting respected authors from France to contribute articles. She wanted the magazine to "raise the intellectual level of the female sex; offer young people useful information that no one thinks to tell them; expose our society's failings; and instil an interest in young women for the life of the mind." Her participation in the National Council of Women of Canada seemed only natural. It was through her magazine that women readers learned about the National Council of Women. French-language newspapers and magazines hardly mentioned the National Council, except to ridicule it or declare that "Its organizers are set on destroying the home and the family." Joséphine used *Le Coin du feu* to challenge clerical opposition to the Council. She wrote, 'Religious questions have absolutely no place on the agenda of the National Council of Women.' Joséphine went on to deplore the limitation of active and high-powered women to passive roles in charitable and religious institutions: "This iron grip will give way under the influence of women like Lady Aberdeen." She supported the social reform ideas then spreading throughout Canada. Invited to speak at the 1894 general meeting of the National Council of Women in Ottawa, Joséphine asked to address the group in French. She was told, "As you like. But your message won't be understood. The provincial delegates do not understand French." Joséphine decided to speak in English and was met with great acclaim.

Lady Julia Drummond (1851-1942) was the first president of the Montreal Local Council of Women from 1893 to 1899, and a member of the Executive Committee of the National Council of Women of Canada in 1907. She was an ardent suffragist.

The third activist in this group was Marie Gérin-Lajoie, a young mother of 26 years of age. After graduating from boarding school at the age of 15, she pursued her own studies in her father's library, training herself in the law. Social injustice was profoundly disturbing to her, and she was particularly concerned about the legal status of married women. She believed it was totally unacceptable for wives to be legally subordinate to their husbands. She insisted that her fiancé, Henri Gérin-Lajoie, accept that after their marriage in 1887, she would dedicate herself to improving the condition of women. Even after the birth of her children, she continued to involve herself in social reform and women's rights work. She published a series of articles in *Le Coin du feu* on the legal status of wives. With regard to Lady Aberdeen, she enthused, "What a woman! Her name will figure among those of the great defenders of our sex."

For Marie Gérin-Lajoie, the creation of the National Council was a godsend and she became an active participant. The president of the Montreal Local, Julia Drummond, was of course an Anglophone. All of these women—Marguerite, Joséphine, Marie, and Julia—had eminent husbands. Marguerite was the wife of a rich industrialist, Rosaire Thibaudeau, owner of Montreal Cotton. Joséphine was the wife of a senator, Raoul Dandurand. Her father, Félix-Gabriel Marchand, would become the premier of Québec in 1897. Marie was the daughter of a judge, Alexandre Lacoste, and the wife of a notable lawyer. Julia was married to the president of the Bank of Montréal. If they had not been members of the social elite, with many servants in their employ, they would never have been able to devote so much time and energy to the cause of women.

The Montreal Local's early achievements included inquiries into the working conditions of women factory workers, the appointment of female inspectors in factories, the separation of young women from "vice-hardened criminals" in the prisons, the founding of reading circles, the organization of public lectures on sanitation, and the opening of the first public baths in Montréal in 1896. Personal hygiene was an important issue for women as they were responsible for caring for the sick and raising healthy families. In 1899, 29 groups were members of the Montreal Local, almost all of them English-speaking and Protestant. A single Catholic group dared to challenge the Archbishop's prohibition: the Dames patronnesses de l'hôpital Notre-Dame. Since this hospital was a secular organization not controlled by the Catholic Church or any other religious institution, it did not come under the authority of the Church.

Was this feminist activism compatible with the Catholic religion? How would the Catholic Church react to these secular organizations?

CHAPTER 3

Christian Feminism and Tensions between Francophone and Anglophone Feminists

AS THE EDITOR of *Le Coin du feu,* Joséphine Marchand-Dandurand was in contact with French women journalists, who introduced her to a Christian feminist magazine, *Le féminisme chrétien*, edited by Marie Maugeret. This discovery was immensely reassuring to Marie Gérin-Lajoie, who worried constantly that religious authorities would view groups devoted to women's rights as a Protestant "aberration." She wrote in her diary, "This discovery has me trembling with delight!"

The word "feminism" arrived in America in 1896, through the Francophone activists of the National Council of Women of Canada. The discovery that feminism was compatible with the Catholic religion spurred Marie Gérin-Lajoie to redouble her efforts. That year, in 1896, the National Council of Women of Canada held its first meeting in French in Montréal. Hundreds of women crowded into the hall.

The response of the press to this meeting was mainly hostile. Families were divided on the subject of feminism. Husbands criticized the members of the National Council, saying, "They are horrible modern women who want to establish female supremacy on Earth!"

It is difficult for us today to comprehend how much courage it took for these women to stand up to the hostility that feminism generated when it first appeared. A female journalist of 1900 declared, "These days, it is not well looked upon to express one's ideas about feminism too openly...."

In 1900, feminists across Canada joined forces to prepare their contribution to the International Exhibition of Paris. They compiled a work that was published in two languages, *Women of Canada: Their Life and Work*, to which many Québec feminists contributed

As their contribution to the International Exhibition of Paris in 1900, the National Council of Women of Canada published a book, *Les Femmes du Canada*, that summarized the achievements and aspirations of Canadian women of the early 20th century. Many Montréal feminists contributed to this book. Published in English and French, it was the first book to provide detailed and accurate information about the condition of women in Canada.

essays. Joséphine Marchand-Dandurand and her husband, Raoul Dandurand, were appointed by the Canadian government as members of Canada's delegation to the Paris exhibition.

In 1901, hundreds of women gathered in a room at the Asile de la Providence in downtown Montréal to hear Joséphine Marchand-Dandurand give a talk entitled *Le féminisme*, in which she described women's central role in society. The feminist movement was clearly here to stay. Women were organizing successfully. Marie Gérin-Lajoie remarked, "It seems that what women needed was strong coordinated action like this … collective action."

In the Anglophone community, where women had been admitted to universities since the early 1870s, and were now working as doctors and scholars, the movement was more developed. French Canadian women realized they had not progressed as much as English-speaking Canadians, who were more highly educated. Also, Ontario law had been reformed in 1872, reducing women's legal dependence upon their husbands.

The right for a woman to be considered a "person" under the law was the great battle that Marie Gérin-Lajoie fought in Québec. In 1903, she published a book, *Traité de droit usuel*, in which she showed how women "abdicated their freedom" when they married. She managed to convince the boarding schools and the higher grades of the public schools to include her textbook in their curriculums. She herself gave dozens of talks on the issue.

Every year, delegates from many Canadian cities gathered for the general meeting of the National Council of Women of Canada (Ottawa, 1898).

Thanks to feminist journalists, increasing numbers of women learned about the social issues connected with feminism. It was one of the burning issues of the early 1900s. Women journalists, such as Françoise (pseudonym of Robertine Barry) in *La Patrie*, Colombine (pseudonym of Éva Circé-Côté) in *Les Débats*, Gaëtane de Montreuil (pseudonym of Georgina Bélanger) in *La Presse,* and Léonise Valois in *Le Monde illustré*, helped spread these new ideas. Beginning in 1902, Robertine Barry published her own magazine, *Le Journal de Françoise*, and was replaced at *La Patrie* by Madeleine Huguenin.

Robertine Barry (1863-1910) was known as a journalist in the early 1900s under the pseudonym of Françoise. Robertine Barry published *Le Journal de Françoise* from 1902 to 1909. She was associated with all the feminist activities in Montréal at the time.

Relations between French-speaking women (Catholics) and English-speaking women (predominately Protestants) were often difficult. French Canadian women had to speak in English during meetings of the Montreal Local. Three episodes contributed to the division between these two "national" groups.

In 1904, a debate was raging in Montréal about the women's vote in the municipal election. Widows and single women, whether home owners or renters, had been entitled to vote at this level of government since 1887. Having no husband, they paid taxes and were therefore considered autonomous under the law. In 1902, Marie Gérin-Lajoie and the members of the Montreal Local won the right to vote for women who were separated. People complained to their city councillors that women generally did not exercise their right to vote, and that these 'immoral women" would vote in their place. Marie Gérin-Lajoie called on the Archbishop to authorize a campaign to encourage Catholic women to vote "so we will not be at the mercy of the Protestants," who had taken it upon themselves to dictate the content of the pamphlets and political platforms proposed to women who were allowed to vote. She launched a powerful press campaign to incite women who could vote (the widows and single women) to exercise their right. On the eve of voting day, the question on everyone's lips was: Will they vote?

The next day, large numbers of women arrived at the polling stations and, calmly and with great dignity, proceeded to cast their votes. On the evening of the election, Marie Gérin-Lajoie expressed her satisfaction: "The ice is broken. I believe we will never go back."

A second instance of this tension occurred in 1905 when the English-speaking community planned to celebrate the centennial of Nelson's victory against Napoleon at Trafalgar. The matrons of the Montreal Local invited their French-speaking sisters to a banquet in honour of the event. These women refused, explaining that they did not want "to celebrate a French defeat."

Lastly, women were anxious to work with the religious orders, which were responsible for so many educational and social institutions, as well as the hospitals. But it was known that the nuns would never agree to take part in a Protestant-dominated organization. On many counts in the early 20th century, French-Canadian nationalism was strong in Québec society. This made Francophone feminists uneasy in the Montreal Local, where they were a minority.

How would Francophone feminists become more autonomous?

CHAPTER 4

The Fédération nationale Saint-Jean-Baptiste

IN THE EARLY 1900S, many Francophone members of the Montreal Local were also members of a new committee of society matrons connected with the Société Saint-Jean-Baptiste, an extremely popular nationalist organization founded in 1834. The wife of the president of this organization, Caroline Dessaulles-Béique, proposed that women organize a massive fundraising campaign in 1903 to repay the debt of the Monument national, a famous theatre on St. Lawrence Boulevard that also hosted free evening classes. The men in the Société Saint-Jean-Baptiste wanted their wives to organize the fundraising campaign because the women had proved themselves to be effective fundraisers for various charities. And, indeed, the campaign was a huge success.

"Our association of society matrons had acquired a certain degree of authority," recalled its president, Caroline Dessaulles-Béique, in her *Mémoires*.

The next step seemed clear to Marie Gérin-Lajoie and Caroline Béique: They would change the goals of this committee, broaden its scope, and set up a federation of Catholic women's groups. They would have to negotiate with the Archbishop of Montréal to obtain permission to establish the new organization.

After two years of preparation and the invaluable support of Joséphine Marchand-Dandurand and Caroline Béique, the first French Canadian women's association was born. On May 26, 1907, at the conclusion of a four-day convention held at the Monument national, women launched their new organization, named after the original committee: the Fédération nationale Saint-Jean-Baptiste (FNSJB). The next day, in an unprecedented move, the daily newspaper *La Patrie* devoted its entire front page to the event. The operation was a resounding success. At last, feminism had taken

Marie Gérin-Lajoie (1868-1945) demanded of her fiancé, Henri Gérin-Lajoie, that he allow her to work freely on improving the condition of women after their marriage. She would only marry on this condition, because this was her life's mission. She founded the Fédération nationale Saint-Jean-Baptiste.

root in Montréal. A decade later, over 30 branches of the FNSJB were established around Montréal. Caroline Béique served as its first president, but everyone knew that Marie Gérin-Lajoie was the true initiator of this huge organization. Now its secretary, she embarked on what would be her life's work. The Fédération's membership included three categories: charitable institutions, consisting primarily of committees of society matrons; educational institutions, including study circles, schools, and the *École ménagère provinciale* [the provincial school of domestic science], founded in 1904; and professional organizations, in the form of labour associations, to improve the conditions of women workers.

As soon as it was founded, 22 groups joined the Fédération. The founders had unanimously decided that "since the Fédération is a sister organization to the Société Saint-Jean-Baptiste, it was only natural that it be composed exclusively of French Canadian women."

The founding of the Fédération nationale Saint-Jean-Baptiste hit the front page of the daily newspaper, *La Patrie*, on May 27, 1907. The article was seven columns wide, a rare occurrence at the time.

Once the founders had obtained the necessary permissions from the Archbishop to set them up, the Federation developed branches in the parishes. The Archbishop assured the founders that the parish priests would facilitate the creation of these branches by reading out their invitation to the congregations on Sunday. Monsignor Bruchési hesitated for a long time before approving the labour associations. But who could resist Marie Gérin-Lajoie? The Archbishop finally stated: "I have no choice but to give my approval. This is the real feminism, because it responds to the needs of our times." As for feminists who demanded women's rights, in his opinion, they were not to be tolerated.

Marie Gérin-Lajoie walked a fine line in everything she undertook. There was widespread disapproval of *le mauvais féminisme* ["bad" or extremist feminism], which promoted women's rights. It is difficult to imagine how much manoeuvring she was forced to do, or all the resistance that she faced. Even her closest associates were fearful. In her diary, she wrote: "Women's social welfare activities were mistakenly seen as manifestations of feminist extremism and individualism, rather than concerned exclusively with the family and society."

Her biggest challenge was to set up the women's labour associations, because the distrust of unions was rampant at this time. Despite everything, Marie Gérin-Lajoie managed to create the *Association des employées de manufactures* [Association of Women Factory Workers], the *Association des employées de magasins* [Association of Women Retail Employees], the *Association des employées de bureaux* [Association of Women Office Workers], the *Association des femmes d'affaires* [Business Women's Association], and the *Association des institutrices* [Association of Women Teachers]. She convinced women workers to sit on the boards of each association and wrote the constitutions herself. It was exhausting work, and despite her dedicated efforts, the newly formed *Association d'aides-domestiques* [Association of Domestic Workers] survived only two years.

Another issue that greatly concerned feminists, including a number of teaching nuns, was higher education for girls. Academic and religious leaders were systematically opposed to the idea because they did not want girls competing with boys. Nevertheless, in April 1908, two determined journalists, Éva Circé-Côté and Gaëtane de Montreuil, decided to bypass the religious authorities and announced the foundation of a secular *lycée* [traditional French secondary school, equivalent to junior college today] in the heart of the students' quarter on Saint Denis Street in Montréal. Young women would be able to continue their studies after graduating from boarding school, and finally have access to university, where they could study the sciences and commerce. They were supported by the *Ligue de l'enseignement,* a group of eminent citizens who wanted to shatter the Church's monopoly on education. Needless to say, this project failed to win over the upstanding members of French-Canadian society.

Marie Gérin-Lajoie's daughter, Marie-Justine, was now 17 and wanted to continue her education and obtain her bachelor's degree.

Where could she study? There were no girls' colleges, and girls were not allowed to go to university. In early 20th century Québec, any change was practically impossible without the permission of religious authorities. Marie Gérin-Lajoie knew this only too well, which is why she would not allow her daughter to attend the secular lycée. Wanting to remain in the good graces of Catholic authorities, Marie Gérin-Lajoie decided to turn to Mother Sainte-Anne-Marie of the Congrégation de Notre-Dame (Montréal's largest teaching order) to find a solution for young women seeking higher education. She believed this was the best way to create an institution where young French Canadian women could earn a bachelor's degree. She challenged the nuns: "The secular group will beat you to it!" She even threatened to send her daughter to study with the Protestants at McGill University.

Following the announcement of the secular lycée's opening, in the spring of 1908, the academic authorities withdrew their objections. Meanwhile—with the Archbishop's endorsement—Mother Saint-Anne-Marie managed to get everything ready for the beginning of classes in a Catholic college in the same year.

The teachers in the new institution were from the university and they were paid $5 per hour, an excellent salary in that era. Classes were given in the Order's motherhouse, the congregation's administrative headquarters, to distinguish it from the girls' boarding schools. It was located in the west end of the city, at the corner of Atwater and Sherbrooke Streets (now Dawson College). It was known as the *École supérieure pour jeunes filles* [Young Ladies' Institute of Higher Learning], and the program was equivalent to the second level of the boys' *collèges classiques*. The nuns were not allowed to use the word "college." That term was reserved for boys' institutions.

In the beginning, there were few students, and not many girls managed to earn their bachelor's degrees. In fact, the nuns themselves attended the classes with their students and then served as coaches. Even the founder, Mother Sainte-Anne-Marie, had to go through the program to earn her BA.

Marie-Justine Gérin-Lajoie graduated in 1911. She was the first French Canadian woman to earn a bachelor's degree. She took first place in the examinations, the *Prix Colin*, ahead of all the young men. This information was quietly withheld, and first prize was awarded to the young man who had come in second. After all, they had to save face for all those gentlemen who had insisted that the female brain was incompatible with higher education.

Still, Mother Sainte-Anne-Marie knew her École supérieure was vulnerable. At every graduation ceremony, political and religious leaders made a point of warning the young women that their diploma did not entitle them to pursue a career. Mother Sainte-Anne-Marie nonetheless informed her new graduates, "If you want to kill the college, go to the university."

As for the secular *lycée*, it struggled for two years, but insufficient funding and the Archbishop's opposition finally forced it to close.

During the following decades, FNSJB feminists relied on the nuns to develop the private secondary school program known as *Lettres-Sciences* [private secondary school program for girls, equivalent to grade 11], colleges, *écoles normales* [private women's teacher training colleges], schools of domestic science and music schools. These nuns, like the feminists, were closely monitored in the programs they were able to offer.

The *École supérieure pour jeunes filles*, whose students promptly joined the FNSJB, was not the only school affiliated with the Fédération. The *École ménagère provinciale*, founded in 1904 by three society matrons of the Société Saint-Jean-Baptiste—supported by their husbands—became the pillar of the educational institutions. At the beginning, its directors were sent to Fribourg, Switzerland for training, after which the school was certified to issue diplomas of domestic science. Although it attracted relatively few full-time domestic science students, the school's evening and Saturday classes were very popular. This school was Québec's modest version of the mission of feminists worldwide to professionalize housework, thus transforming it into a respected occupation. These were the same years in which American women created home economics programs to protest the denigration of their domestic responsibilities and their inferior status in the family.

Many women in early 20th century Québec were determined to explore new avenues and assume new social responsibilities. Christian feminism offered them stimulating opportunities, which is why they adopted it with such enthusiasm.

What were the main activities of these Montréal feminists?

CHAPTER 5

Feminists Hard at Work

THE FÉDÉRATION NATIONALE Saint-Jean-Baptiste (FNSJB) had just been founded and its members were already busy on several fronts, including the campaign against alcohol abuse and infant mortality. No matter how lofty the speeches vaunting the merits of the Canadian family, they were empty words if no steps were taken to reduce the *abus de force* [abuse of superior strength, the timid term used by feminists to refer to wife battering] committed by drunken fathers. And what about the babies who were dying due to poverty and their mothers' ignorance?

According to Marie Gérin-Lajoie, "The cruel and heartbreaking truth is that our babies are dying in numbers, not unlike those in barbaric societies."

In 1907, a temperance committee was formed. Feminists emphasized that in Montréal there were four times as many drinking establishments as bakeries, and proposed an amendment to the *Licenses Act* to block the opening of new taverns. After collecting 60,000 signatures, they took their petition to Québec City, where they presented it to Premier Lomer Gouin. Women from the Montreal Local, who had joined the Fédération in the petition campaign, went with them.

Two men were needed to transport the petition, which was rolled on a wooden cylinder. After much discussion and a counter-petition presented by the liquor merchants, an amendment similar to the women's proposal was finally passed. The provincial treasurer declared, "A principle that has been endorsed by the nation's women will surely be a guarantee of moral reform and progress."

After the passage of this amendment, in fact, the number of *buvettes* [taprooms] in Montréal decreased considerably. Some

people now admitted that perhaps it was a good thing that women were getting involved in politics.

Their victory generated an excessive workload for Fédération members, however. They now had to monitor the municipal permits registry. As soon as a liquor licence application was submitted, they also had to collect signatures to prevent the establishment from opening. The Fédération performed this thankless task until 1921, when the sale of alcohol came under provincial jurisdiction.

Initiatives concerning infant mortality came from several sources, because many sectors were involved in this issue: doctors, the Church, the government, women, and more specifically feminists. The poor quality of milk was identified as one of the main culprits. In the early 1900s, the pasteurization of milk had not yet become compulsory. Especially in the summertime, thousands of children became ill and died. In 1901, two pasteurized milk depots were opened in Montréal. The depot serving the English-speaking community was run by the Montreal Foundling and Baby Hospital. French-speaking Quebecers used a service called Gouttes de lait

Early 20th century feminists were associated with the creation of *Gouttes de lait* [Drops of Milk], groups that distributed pasteurized milk to young families and organized public talks on hygiene and childrearing.

that had been started by a small group of physicians. The journalist Madeleine Huguenin persuaded her employers at *La Patrie* to fund the Francophone initiative, but, she succeeded for only five months. The founding of a children's hospital, Sainte-Justine Hospital, in 1907, led to the permanent establishment of Gouttes de lait in 1910. A second Gouttes de lait service later opened in a working class parish. It was the start of what was to become an influential movement. From 1914 to 1916, the Fédération worked with physicians to form a network in Montréal. They raised funds to hire a woman to coordinate the network, but the money quickly ran out. It appeared that the doctors were less than enthusiastic about women from the Fédération taking leadership.

In 1912, Caroline Leclerc-Hamilton created *Assistance maternelle* [Maternal Aid] in Montréal, an agency that provided services to working class mothers, including childbirth services, the distribution of layettes, and childcare advice. The service grew considerably, expanding to other cities in Québec. This group also joined the Fédération.

Domestic service was another concern of the Fédération. Fédération members required household staff so they could devote themselves to their activist work, and they were dissatisfied with the training their servants were receiving. Because the École ménagère provinciale's program was inadequate, they organized classes for domestic workers. Fédération women set up a home for young women who arrived in Montréal from the countryside to find work as servants, as well as a welcome booth for them in the railway stations.

All these services needed to be expanded to the parishes; women had to be recruited to manage them and they had to be provided with training. In the labour associations, women organized home economics classes and refresher training, insurance services, and campaigns to improve working conditions, for example, chairs for shopgirls and support for women teachers in their campaign to change their profoundly discriminatory pension plan. At the turn of the century, 94 retired male teachers and 19 teachers' widows shared 53 per cent of the fund, while 462 retired female teachers had to divide up the rest. There were documents to prepare for the inquiries on industrial labour and public lecture series to organize on the rights of married women, sanitation, and children's health.

The Fédération now had an office that was open to the public every afternoon, six days a week. Most of those knocking on the doors were women in distress; women volunteers tried to direct them to the appropriate services. The Fédération organized a big fundraising campaign to assist various charities in the city. They published a directory of these agencies to inform the public of the available services. These groundbreaking initiatives were all conducted entirely by Fédération volunteers.

Fédération activists partnered with activists from the Montreal Local under certain circumstances, in particular, the movement against alcoholism. But here the gap between the two organizations began to widen. The Fédération opposed total prohibition, while the Montreal Local was affiliated with the Woman's Christian Temperance Union which staunchly advocated prohibition. At the first meeting of the FNSJB's temperance committee, Madame Leman, the chair of the committee, made sure to have it noted in the minutes that whatever happened, she wanted to be able to continue enjoying her glass of port.

Further, when the Fédération fought for protective measures for female workers, the Montreal Local opposed this strategy, claiming that it was illogical to demand sexual equality and at the same time demand protective measures like the prohibition of night shifts for women. In 1912, the National Council of Women of Canada adopted a list of official demands, called the "Women's Platform." Among the issues it addressed were the "age of consent" (age at which a girl is considered legally able to consent to sexual relations), prostitution, the abandonment of wives by their husbands, and the equal rights of mothers. In Québec, Fédération members rarely discussed these issues, so popular with other Canadian women, because Catholic women were under constant surveillance. After their 1911 convention, the bishop would not even allow them to publish a text about the work that the Miséricorde nuns were doing with unwed mothers.

The National Council of Women was affiliated with the International Council of Women, while the Fédération joined the International Union of Catholic Women's Leagues. And when Carrie Derick, president of the Montreal Local, invited Emmeline Pankhurst, the English suffragist famous for her sensational actions,

Fédération members prudently stayed away.

The Fédération's motto was "justice through charity," reflecting the fact that this feminist organization had rapidly adopted a charitable, rather than an activist, orientation. This trend was accentuated in the years to come, as Fédération activists found themselves cornered by the notion of the "bad feminism" that was being propagated by religious authorities.

Marie Gérin-Lajoie explained why they made so many compromises: "In certain circles our ideas were considered so scandalous that without the backing of the bishop and several other members of the clergy, we would have been social outcasts."

What was French Canadian society's response to feminism? Certainly, after two decades, feminism was an established force in the province, though mainly in Montréal. The Quebec Local, founded in Québec City in 1894, was unable to gain a firm footing or obtain the bishop's endorsement, and, in 1900, was forced to close its doors. The main impact of early 20th century feminism was that women had shown that you didn't have to become a nun to be socially active.

Feminists believed that women should do this work, not the Church or the State, two male dominated institutions. Though their aspirations did not achieve concrete form, they did succeed in proposing new ways of organizing social assistance. They were bold enough to take on religious and political leaders directly in order to promote their ideas. When she learned that Sir Wilfrid Laurier, the future Prime Minister of Canada, opposed women's suffrage, Marie Gérin-Lajoie declared that she hoped that feminists would change his mind.

Increasingly, Catholic and Protestant feminists alike were coming to the same conclusion: "If we had the vote, it would be so much easier!" At the dawn of the 20th century, only a few feminists were demanding political equality. Now, most of them wanted the vote. They had seen that by organizing on their own, outside the control of the clergy and other men, they were much more effective. But winning the vote and wielding direct power was something else again.

How would feminists fight for the right to vote?

WOMEN ORGANIZE

1893   Creation of the National Council of Women of Canada
by Lady Aberdeen

1893   Creation of the Montreal Local Council of Women,
member of the NCWC

1900   Participation of Canadian feminists in the International
Exhibition of Paris

1907   Founding of the Fédération nationale Saint-Jean-Baptiste
by Marie Gérin-Lajoie and Caroline Béique

1908   Founding of the École supérieure pour jeunes filles by
Mother Sainte-Anne-Marie

2 | FEMINIST CAMPAIGN FOR WOMEN'S VOTING RIGHTS 1913-1940

CHAPTER 6

Montreal Suffrage Association and Opposition
to the Women's Vote

Ligues à
Rome,
see p. 54

THE NEXT DEVELOPMENTS in Québec and English Canada closely mirrored those in many other countries. By 1912, women's suffrage had become a central theme in many countries.

Since 1908, the British suffragist movement had been conducting a spectacular campaign for women's suffrage. When they realized that persuasion and discussions with members of Parliament were leading nowhere, British suffragists changed tactics, not hesitating to break the law in their quest for the vote. Suffragists chained themselves to fences and were arrested and jailed. The suffragists regularly made the headlines, especially in their confrontations with the police. Many were imprisoned and led hunger strikes. The authorities force-fed them, provoking renewed demonstrations demanding their release. Large scale demonstrations were held in Britain between 1910 and 1914.

In 1913, Emily Wilding Davison, an Englishwoman who believed in self-sacrifice for the cause, threw herself under the horses at the Derby race track. This dramatic suicide of a feminist activist caused a sensation. On the day of her funeral a gigantic march was held in London. Why are we today unaware of the sacrifice of Emily Wilding Davison?

In Canada, the movement was far less sensational, but suffragists nonetheless made the news almost every day. In early 1913, inspired by their British counterparts, Canadian feminists launched a major campaign for women's suffrage. This was also the moment that the journalist Henri Bourassa—at the height of his popularity after founding the nationalist daily, *Le Devoir*, in 1910— entered the public debate in Québec. He was a fierce opponent of feminism and published a series of articles on the subject in 1913. He

Carrie Derick (1862-1941) was the first Canadian woman to become a university professor. She was president of the Montreal Suffrage Association. She was a fervent advocate of sexual equality.

adamantly believed that feminism was a menace to the family and French Canadian society. In his opinion, feminism was a Protestant aberration, as bad as socialism. Anti-feminism had its first Québec champion in Bourassa.

In the same year, women with the Montreal Local created the Montreal Suffrage Association. Carrie Derick, Canada's first female university professor, became its president. The group produced a play, organized a film screening, circulated petitions, and wrote letters to the different levels of government. They protested the treatment of British suffragists: "They have reinstituted medieval torture, and it is a violation of the traditional principles of British justice."

They set up booths in downtown Montréal to inform the public about the issue of women's suffrage. In November, *The Montreal Herald*, the only Montréal newspaper in favour of women's suffrage, published a special issue and had women sell it in the streets. It created a scandal.

In 1913, the Fédération nationale Saint-Jean-Baptiste launched a new magazine, *La Bonne Parole* [The Good Word]. Faced with the nationalists' opposition to feminism, Marie Gérin-Lajoie opted for prudence. The articles were extremely moderate in tone and steered away from mentioning women's suffrage.

In the summer of 1914, war began in Europe and eventually involved the rest of the world. People hoped it would end quickly, but it dragged on for four long years. It was the "Great War," or the First World War. Though women's suffrage was no longer in the headlines, the Montreal Suffrage Association continued campaigning. Women threw themselves into the Canadian war effort, fundraising for the Red Cross, assisting prisoners, preparing packages, and making bandages.

Women were needed to work in many sectors, especially in the arms industry, to replace the men who had gone to fight in Europe. Canadian feminists, who were traditionally non-partisan, found it hard not to take sides with the political parties. They were deeply divided on a number of questions, including unionization of women workers, the women's vote, and the compulsory drafting of young men, conscription. In 1916, Emily Murphy, a feminist from western Canada, sparked a wave of protest when she suggested that only women of British descent should be granted the vote!

Henri Bourassa's reaction was an indication that public opinion was now shifting against feminism. Until then, the authorities had ignored their actions, considering the feminist movement harmless. Now, feminism was perceived as a dangerous movement. For several years, even *bon féminisme* became suspect. In the press, new women journalists replaced the original leaders and the tone changed significantly. They urged women to resist feminism—and some did. In *Le Devoir*, Fadette (pseudonym of Henriette Dessaulles, Henri Bourassa's cousin) implored women not to set themselves up as men's rivals. In the pages of *La Presse*, Colette (pseudonym of Édouardina Lesage) insisted on the polarization between feminists and "real women." The galvanizing articles of Joséphine Dandurand and Robertine Barry were a thing of the past; Joséphine was ill and had retired from public life and Robertine had died in 1910.

The opponents of feminism seemed to have no idea of what feminists were really thinking. They believed that women wanted to take men's places, when just the opposite was true: feminists wanted more rights in order to better carry out their "womanly and maternal roles." At the time, this vision, much more than the ideal of sexual equality, motivated their activism.

Increasingly, the fact that women were organizing in autonomous organizations was perceived as menacing. This was the context when, in 1915, the Ministry of Agriculture established the *Cercles de fermières*, to encourage women to oppose the rural exodus to the cities. Similar associations, known as Women's Institutes, had already been formed in English Canada.

The Cercles de fermières became popular with rural women who, until that point, had kept their distance from the feminist movement. Two years after its inception, ten Cercles de fermières had already appeared in different regions of Québec. This group provided rural women with opportunities they had never before had, including the chance simply to get out of the home for a while. Meetings were held on Sundays, before or after Mass, attended by countless women. The Ministry of Agriculture distributed eggs, seeds, and beehives to encourage women to take up poultry farming, horticulture, and beekeeping—the "feminine" forms of agriculture. Women were invited to attend crafts and cooking classes. One of the Cercles' founders, the agronomist Georges Bouchard, reassured those who were worried about this new association: "Those who fear their daughters will turn into suffragists or 'emancipated women' just have to see how the Cercles operate ... and their fears will disappear."

The groups operated under the firm hand of the Ministry of Agriculture. While the Women's Institutes supported many feminist goals, the Cercles de fermières were much more conservative and even opposed feminist demands.

Meanwhile, the Montreal Suffrage Association continued its activist campaign, though their actions were much less dramatic than those of the British suffragists. They went to the Edinburg Café every day where for three hours they would sit, hand out leaflets and books, and inform women about the aberrations of the *Civil Code of Québec* and the working conditions of women factory workers. They sold 3,000 copies of an informational booklet about women's legal status. They also organized public lectures in partnership with other

Canadian women's suffrage organizations.

Women's rights to vote in a provincial election depended on the laws in that particular province. During the First World War, some Canadian provinces passed women's suffrage legislation. Women in Manitoba, Saskatchewan and Alberta got the vote in 1916; and in 1917, it was granted to women in British Columbia and Ontario. Women were elected as members of provincial legislatures and even appointed as ministers in some provinces.

In Québec, however, male politicians, journalists, and bishops were unanimously opposed to women obtaining the vote. Legal experts were especially virulent in their opposition. They believed that allowing women the right to vote was counter to the *Civil Code* in force in Québec. Large numbers of women were also against women's suffrage.

What would put a dent in this opposition?

CHAPTER 7

The Right to Vote in Federal Elections

IN JULY 1917, the federal government—instead of relying on volunteers to bolster the armed forces—passed a conscription bill that made it compulsory for young men to be drafted into the armed forces. In Québec, this law met with strong opposition and angry demonstrations. Nationalists were unwilling "to die for England." The opponents of conscription threatened to bring down the Conservative government. Prime Minister Borden ushered in the *War-time Elections Act*, which, among other things, gave voting rights to women who had a son or husband on active duty. Since English Canadians comprised the majority of the armed forces, their mothers and wives, most of whom were more in agreement with government policies on the war, were the ones who would be able to vote.

This law inspired Marie Gérin-Lajoie to break her silence on women's suffrage. She wrote to the Canadian prime minister: "We demand that [all] women be entitled to vote in federal elections, just like men, in acknowledgement of the immense contributions they have made during the war: helping the wounded, especially in the Red Cross, and conducting humanitarian work that is a tribute to the country."

She also addressed her readers in *La Bonne Parole*: "The partial vote that women have just been granted is more of an insult than a tribute, because what it really does is give some soldiers the right to vote several times through the intermediary of their female relatives."

In protest, she published in *La Bonne Parole* the names of the members who voted "for" and "against" the bill. Feminists should know both who their allies and their enemies are. Many English Canadian feminists also protested. It was now just a matter of time before all women would have the vote. Attitudes were beginning to change.

The following year, on March 20, 1918, Prime Minister Borden introduced legislation to amend the new election act by giving all adult women who were born or naturalized British subjects the right to vote in federal elections. Despite vehement opposition, mainly from Québec's MPs, the bill passed. At last, women in Québec could vote, but just in federal elections.

Because the public's attention was focussed on the endless war in Europe, newspapers barely covered this event. Conscription had become a national crisis, leading to a deadly riot in Québec City. Henri Bourassa was the lone voice protesting women's newly won right to vote in a series of articles with provocative titles such as: "Brains in Disarray—Triumph of Democracy," "The Right to Vote —The Battle of the Sexes—Will We Let Our Women Be Degraded?" and "Women's Political Influence: Advanced Countries—Women Wear the Pants."

These articles signalled that it would be difficult for Québec women to win the vote in provincial elections, since it was viewed as a menace to the all important French Canadian Catholic "difference." Nationalists unanimously opposed the women's vote. The official line was to extol the woman's role as mother. In 1918, a priest promoted "the revenge of the cradles," which would enable French Canadians to maintain their high numbers and influence within Canada. He concluded that it was women's nationalist duty to make babies.

In contrast, Montréal feminists—like feminists throughout Canada—were thrilled that Canada was now one of the few countries to grant women the right to vote. It was not until 1920, after a memorable struggle, that women in the United States won this right. Women in Great Britain had to wait until 1928, and it wasn't until 1944 that French women finally won the vote. Aboriginal women and men and women of Asian origin, however, did not have the right to vote in Canada until after World War II.

During the next federal election in 1921, women voted for the first time. In Montréal, the Fédération nationale Saint-Jean-Baptiste took this new civic duty very seriously. It organized political education classes for women that were given at the Université de Montréal, reflecting the importance attached to ensuring that women could fully exercise this right. Naturally, the organizers had first ensured the legitimacy of their endeavour by obtaining an endorsement from religious authorities.

Unfortunately, only women who lived in Montréal could attend the classes. Hundreds of women crammed into the lectures, which were strictly non-partisan: the idea was simply to make women aware of their new political responsibilities. On voting day, contrary to the prediction that women's presence in the polling stations would cause chaos, women voters turned out in large numbers and there were no unfortunate incidents.

What would women need to do to win the provincial vote in Québec?

CHAPTER 8

First Expedition to Québec City

FEMINISTS IN QUÉBEC knew they would now have to continue the battle for the vote at the provincial level. In 1922, thanks to the persuasive powers of a new young member of the Fédération nationale Saint-Jean-Baptiste named Idola Saint-Jean, a new women's suffrage organization was born. The *Comité du suffrage provincial* [Provincial Suffrage Committee], a bilingual group, was chaired by two women: Marie Gérin-Lajoie and Anna Lyman, then president of the Women's Club. Idola Saint-Jean, who was more progressive in her thinking than Marie Gérin-Lajoie, acted as secretary. Excitement was in the air as the women discussed a proposal to send a women's suffrage delegation to Québec City.

"Is it the right time to act?" asked some women.

"Yes," answered Anna Lyman, who had been told by a member of the National Assembly that Premier Taschereau was favourable to the idea.

"Are we ready?" they asked.

"No!" insisted several Anglophone women, thinking that the numbers of French Canadian women who wanted the vote were still insufficient.

"Yes!" answered Marie Gérin-Lajoie.

Convinced that the time was ripe, she told the women she had the support of a woman in the leadership of the Cercles de fermières, an association known for its opposition to women's suffrage.

After much lively discussion, the majority of the Committee members decided to organize a dramatic event to convince the provincial government that, given that women were entitled to vote in federal elections, they should also have the right to vote in Québec.

An active member of the Fédération nationale Saint-Jean-Baptiste from its inception, Idola Saint-Jean (1880-1945) took part in the women's suffrage campaign and in 1927, founded the Alliance canadienne pour le vote des femmes du Québec. She wrote a bilingual column on women's rights for the *Montreal Herald* in 1929, and, beginning in 1933, published the magazine *La Sphère féminine*. She ran in the federal election campaign of 1931, winning 3,000 votes.

On February 9, 1922, a delegation of over 500 women arrived in Québec City to support a women's suffrage bill. Marie Gérin-Lajoie, Idola Saint-Jean and a newcomer, Thérèse Casgrain, addressed the lawmakers on behalf of French-speaking women, Carrie Derick, Dr. Grace Ritchie-England, and Julia Drummond spoke on behalf of English-speaking women. The MNAs and Premier Alexandre Taschereau listened politely as the women gave their speeches. Premier Taschereau spoke as soon as the women had finished, stating that he believed Québec women would doubtless have the vote one day, but his government would not be the one to grant it. It was a crushing blow. Not surprisingly, given the Premier's response to their demands, the bill failed to pass.

The action awakened the anti-feminists again. The bishops proclaimed their opposition to the women's vote, especially the

Thérèse Forget-Casgrain (1896-1981) made a name for herself among feminists in 1922, when she addressed the Legislative Assembly on behalf of a women's delegation that had gone to Québec City to formally demand the vote.

bishop of Québec City, Monsignor Roy. A petition was circulated, signed by 30,000 women who affirmed they did not want the vote. Anti-women's suffrage articles appeared in *La Bonne Fermière*, a magazine addressed to the Cercles de fermières. *Le Devoir* published the opinions of "anti-suffragists." An article by the Dean of Laval University, Louis-Adolphe Paquet, attempted to make theological and philosophical arguments to support his claim "that feminism is a perverse movement that menaces the foundations of the family and society."

Infuriated by the tone of this campaign denigrating the women's suffrage movement, and especially angered by the bishops, Marie Gérin-Lajoie asked the advice of the Pope's representative, Pietro du Maria.

"But you don't have to answer to the bishop of Québec," he responded. "Carry on!"

She decided to go to Rome and obtain directives from the Pope himself. The bishop of Québec was furious and accused her of "trying to set up a Church within the Church." But Marie Gérin-Lajoie was determined to go to Rome and participate in the convention of the International Union of Catholic Women's League.

Would this stunning initiative produce the desired result?

CHAPTER 9

Convention in Rome

MARIE GÉRIN-LAJOIE had made a smart move when she made the Fédération nationale Saint-Jean-Baptiste a member of the International Union of Catholic Women's Leagues way back in 1911. She went to the convention, accompanied by the FNSJB's secretary, Georgette Lemoine. Most of the delegates were from France, Italy, Spain, Poland, and Germany. The convention was chaired by a Polish countess. The proceedings were held in French. Committees were focussing on the "propagation of the [Catholic] faith," the "white slave trade," and "the immorality of fashion and the cinema." Marie Gérin-Lajoie made sure she was on the Political Committee.

She was delighted when, after lengthy discussion, the Political Committee adopted the following two motions:

> 1. That Catholic women of all countries understand their moral responsibility in the face of the vote, regardless of the form it may take; and
> 2. That women must prepare for their new mission [the vote] by taking moral, religious and civic instruction.

This was a major reversal. The Church had always been opposed to women exercising the right to vote. Why had the Church changed its position? The war of 1914-1918 had transformed Europe's political landscape. More than that, the Communist Revolution of 1917 in Russia was viewed as a threat by the Catholic Church and several European governments.

These political upheavals were accompanied by an unprecedented cultural change of modernism that affected women's lives in the 1920s. Contemporary fashion represented social change, as women began wearing short dresses and showing bare legs in public

Founded in 1910, the International Union of Catholic Women's Leagues held a major convention in Rome in 1922. Marie Gérin-Lajoie went to the convention hoping for papal directives concerning women's suffrage.

for the first time. Embracing their newly found freedom, young women eagerly adopted this modern trend, delighted to be rid of the long dresses that swept up the filth on the sidewalks and floors. Women cut their hair fashionably short, adopting a new style, *à la garçonne*, urchin style. In men's minds, this was really stepping over the line. But women didn't stop there: They wore make-up and began wearing pants to play sports. Cinema, jazz, the automobile, fashionable new dances — all forms of modernity were attacks on morality in the eyes of religious leaders.

Even the attitudes of the Church seemed to have changed somewhat. The Catholic Church decided it needed the support of women to help stop the growing influence of communism in Europe and of modernism in general. This was what motivated Pope Benedict XV and his successor, Pius XI, to change the Catholic Church's position on women's suffrage. The Pope hoped that women would vote against the Communist parties and throw their support behind the Catholic parties. Seen from this perspective, voting could even be considered the duty of every good Catholic woman. It seemed that official Church doctrine would no longer stand in the way of women getting the vote.

But this almost victory was short-lived. Just as the Rome convention's closing plenary began, Marie Gérin-Lajoie discovered to her horror that a "third proposal" had been added:

3. That women in every country submit in advance any new initiative in the area of women's suffrage for the approval of the episcopate [the bishops in each country].

Marie was thunderstruck. Who could have added this new motion? She tried, without success, to have it struck. Later, she learned that it was the work of a Roman prelate who had spoken with Henri Bourassa, who was in Rome on a visit, as it happened. Bourassa had convinced him to add the third proposal, arguing that women's suffrage would have a harmful effect on the political situation in many countries, and saying: "As destructive as the horrors of 1914-1918 were [in Europe], the women's vote is not justified [in our country].

A bishop in Québec later declared, "The women's vote, which might be useful to the Church in other countries, would be of no value here at this time."

On his return from Rome in June 1922, Henri Bourassa's first action was to print the infamous third proposal on the first page of *Le Devoir*.

Discouraged, Marie Gérin-Lajoie resigned from her position as chair of the Comité du suffrage provincial as soon as she returned to Montréal. She nevertheless continued her educational work to raise women's awareness about feminism. At the same time, she wrangled from Msgr. Gauthier, the Bishop of Montréal, the right to continue giving political education classes to women. In this way, she hoped to promote women's suffrage indirectly. In the end, the Bishop would only allow her to do it in her own name, not under the auspices of the FNSJB.

Unperturbed, she carried on, seizing every opportunity to raise the issue of women's right to participate in political life: the appointment of a women to the *Conseil de l'instruction publique* [Public Education Council]; municipal elections in which widows and single women were entitled to vote; and the creation of a Commission to regulate women's work. In response to repeated feminist urgings that the provincial government institute pensions for needy mothers, Premier Taschereau exclaimed, "If we give women the vote, we'll have to give mothers a pension!"

In 1926, a delegation of suffragists travelled to Québec City, hoping to present their point of view to a committee. After making the women wait from morning until midnight, the committee further humiliated the group by refusing to let them speak. Marie dug in her heels, determined not to give up. She continued to participate on an individual basis in the rare meetings of the Comité du suffrage provincial, and sent countless requests for a meeting with Msgr. Gauthier to persuade him to change his mind. The Bishop did not deign to answer her letters. In 1928, at the annual general meeting of Assistance Maternelle, he proclaimed, "Feminism is a disease that must be cured by actions other than politics; one or two female elected representatives will not solve anything."

The following day, the newspapers read: "Women must desert politics and devote themselves to charity."

From 1922 to 1928, Marie Gérin-Lajoie ceaselessly pressed the bishop for approval to promote women's suffrage. At the same time, she dedicated herself to consolidating the Fédération nationale Saint-Jean-Baptiste. She bought a house for the Fédération and organized fundraising campaigns to furnish and equip the premises. Here, she held meetings, classes, and lectures. The Fédération house was a beehive of activity. The FNSJB magazine, *La Bonne Parole*, was supported by the Soeurs du Bon-Conseil, the religious order founded by Marie Gérin-Lajoie's daughter, Marie-Justine, now Sister Gérin-Lajoie. In 1929, Marie Gérin-Lajoie finally withdrew from the women's suffrage campaign, although she kept up her other feminist activism. She was 62 and had been fighting the same battle for 36 years.

Who would now take on the feminist leadership role?

CHAPTER 10

Two New Feminist Associations

THÉRÈSE CASGRAIN TOOK OVER as president of the Comité du suffrage provincial in 1927. Idola Saint-Jean, who had more or less founded this group, believed it was not representative enough because its membership was mainly composed of upper middle class women. She decided to establish the *Alliance canadienne pour le vote des femmes du Québec* and was very proud when she recruited over 300 Montréal women to her new group, most of them working class women. In 1928, Thérèse Casgrain changed the name of the Comité du suffrage provincial to the *Ligue des droits de la femme* [Women's Rights League] and broadened its goals, calling for amendments to the *Civil Code of Québec* and the right of women to practise law. The League had only a few dozen members. Fortunately, the two new groups worked together. Both welcomed women from all faiths. Catholic and Protestant women worked side by side, and like their sisters at the Fédération, all the women worked on a volunteer basis. The presidents of these two associations, Thérèse Casgrain and Idola Saint-Jean, became the principal spokeswomen of the feminist movement.

Back in 1915, the government had responded to the creation of the first suffragist association by setting up the Cercles de fermières. This time, the Catholic Church orchestrated the counter-offensive, by encouraging the formation of a new women's association. It created the *Ligue féminine catholique* [Catholic Women's League] in 1929, a group dedicated to the promotion of female modesty— no short sleeves, no bare arms, no low necklines and no make-up— and to Catholic morals. It was remarkably successful at recruiting women, boasting 2,000 members at its inception and 70,000 by 1932.

At the same time an association of *amicales* [alumnae clubs composed of graduates of Catholic boarding schools] was founded, called the *Association fédérée des anciennes élèves des couvents catholiques du Canada* [Canadian Federation of Former Pupils of Catholic Convent Schools]. This initiative came from women in Ontario, who wanted an organization like the English-Canadian women's alumnae clubs. Since most women completed their short educational careers in boarding schools, this association also succeeded in attracting a large membership. In 1933, over 170 *amicales* joined the new association, representing 35,400 members. Women in these alumnae clubs essentially devoted themselves to charitable endeavours, distancing themselves from controversial women's rights issues. Society dictated that a woman must perform her womanly role. This federation survived only a short time. It ceased operating in the mid 1930s, because the bishops and religious orders wanted to be independent of an Ontario-based organization. The *amicales*, however, continued to be active in each boarding school.

Feminists were not deterred from their goals by the emergence of these Catholic anti-feminist groups. Every year, the League and the Alliance would persuade an MNA from the governing party to present a women's suffrage bill to the Québec National Assembly. Every year, they made their *pélerinage* [pilgrimage] to Québec City to sit in the visitors' gallery and listen while the politicians debated the bill. Year after year, they were subjected to the same drivel. It was back to square one every time. They were still being derisively labelled "suffragettes."

"I may be a feminist, but I'm not a suffragette!" said Thérèse Casgrain. "We must be moderate, reasonable, and serene when we present our demands." She put this into practice when she sent Premier Taschereau 63 roses on his birthday in 1929. When she presented her case, she always invoked justice, law, logic, and the evolution of democracy.

Her colleague, Idola Saint-Jean, was slightly more radical. She hoped that "Man will abolish the last surviving form of aristocracy: the aristocracy of the sexes." She did not use the word *sexism*, because it had not yet been invented. But she clearly believed that male supremacy was the source of the injustices feminists were denouncing.

The government set up the Dorion Commission in 1929 to examine the question of the rights of married women, perhaps a gesture by the premier to make up for his opposition to women's suffrage. All the feminist associations, including the FNSJB and Marie Gérin-Lajoie, presented briefs at the public hearings in Montréal and Québec City. The Ligue des droits de la femme, the Alliance canadienne pour le vote des femmes du Québec, and the Montreal Local also took part. For Marie Gérin-Lajoie, it was the culmination of a personal campaign of more than 30 years. In 1926, the deplorable situation of married women—who did not even have the right to open a bank account in their own name—had elicited this outburst from her: "Québec is the laughing-stock of the world!"

Feminist groups demanded amendments to several articles of the *Civil Code of Québec* to eliminate the legal subordination of wives. They backed up their demands with detailed draft amendments. Their language was direct. They used strong words such as "yoke" (Marie Gérin-Lajoie), "slavery" (Idola Saint-Jean), and "abuses" (Thérèse Casgrain).

When the Dorion Commission's report came out in 1931, only a few of the feminists' demands had been adopted: women's right to keep their own paycheque instead of handing it over to their husbands and the right of wives who separated from their husbands to maintain custody of their children and to benefit from stronger legal protections.

The commissioners refused to abolish the legal subordination of wives and the "double standard" law. This was an article in the *Civil Code* under which a woman could not ask for a separation for adultery, unless the husband brought his mistress to live in the family home, while the husband could obtain a separation for adultery at any time. According to the commissioners: "The injury to the husband is greater, and it is easier for a wife to pardon her husband."

Would feminists be discouraged by this setback?

CHAPTER 11

The Great Depression

THE 1930S WERE HARD, due to the economic crisis known as the Great Depression. The women's suffrage campaign continued, but was constantly eclipsed by the economic crisis. The unemployment rate skyrocketed, surpassing 33 per cent. Poverty—indeed, extreme poverty—was a reality in every city. New political movements like socialism and communism, until then considered to be European-based movements, began to develop in Québec. Another political current, fascism, appeared in Italy and later also grew popular in Québec. Many people were seeking a new social and political order.

THE FIRST REFUGE FOR WOMEN AND CHILDREN

With no social safety net on which to fall back, many people were barely surviving. Single women were especially vulnerable. Yvonne de Maisonneuve founded a new charity in 1932, a home for "women who are worn out and unemployed, young women freshly arrived from the country, ladies in distress who were duped by an unscrupulous pseudo fiancé, and girls carrying an unwanted child who are trying to hide their bulging bellies." She surrounded herself with associates who were neither nuns nor society matrons. Every year, most of these women renewed their commitment to the charity and its work.

Solidarité féminine, a women's group affiliated with the Communist Party, made its appearance during the economic crisis of the 1930s. In 1937, municipal authorities decided to cut the numbers of people who were entitled to assistance. Solidarité féminine protested by occupying the office of Montréal City Council. The action made front page news in *La Patrie*.

Yet, Yvonne de Maisonneuve was unable to obtain the endorsement of the Church, either for her group or for the home she had just opened. Municipal authorities used this lack of Church endorsement as an excuse not to fund the shelter. Without public funding, how was she going to take care of all the women and children who

EDITION QUOTIDIENNE

La Patrie

2¢

59e ANNEE — Temps probable demain: BEAU ET CHAUD — MONTREAL, VENDREDI 18 JUIN 1937 — Le soleil se lève à 4 h. 11 (h.a.) et se couche à 7 h. 51 (h.a.) — No 97

LES 4,000 MISÉREUX
ASSURÉS DE LEURS SECOURS

(LIRE EN PAGE 3)

Mort subite de M. Gaston Doumergue

(LIRE EN PAGE 24)

Les femmes réclament du pain à l'hôtel de ville

Photographies prises, hier après-midi, lors de la grève sur le tas d'une centaine de femmes, dirigées par M. Candide Rochefort, député de Sainte-Marie, dans la salle du conseil municipal. (1) Le maire Adhémar Raynault tente de calmer les récalcitrantes et leur promet qu'il va faire l'impossible pour leur donner satisfaction. (2) Mlle Pauline Tremblay lance: "Je ne retourne pas chez nous sans avoir l'assurance que nous allons avoir du secours!" (3) Une pauvre mère s'affaisse, pendant que le maire discute avec l'échevin Emile Dubreuil. Ses compagnes se portent à son secours. (4) Un groupe de femmes qui ont envahi la salle du conseil et se sont installées dans les fauteuils des échevins. (Photo la "Patrie").

were living in her house? She decided to approach the suppliers of food and utilities directly, to keep the home in operation, first on Fairmount Street, then on La Gauchetière Street. This was the first non-religious (or secular) shelter in Québec for women and children in need. Known as Notre-Dame de la Protection, it was the forerunner of Le Chaînon, a well-known refuge in Montréal today. Though it didn't define itself as such, its mission was decidedly feminist: to support women who were victims of a social order dominated by men. In this shelter, all women were welcome, no questions asked—a revolutionary concept for the times. According to our standards today, this was a feminist organization, but Yvonne de Maisonneuve would have been very surprised to hear it.

RIGHTS OF WOMEN WORKERS

The labour associations created by the FNSJB in 1907 had failed to adapt, either to the new economic context of the Depression or to the appearance of Catholic trade unions in 1921. They opposed using strikes as a pressure tactic. Their membership, which in the early 1920s had surpassed 800, fell considerably after 1930.

During this period, a group of working class women began organizing in a group associated with the Communist Party called Solidarité féminine. They organized several high profile actions: an occupation of the streetcars, a demonstration outside City Hall, and disruptions of political meetings. Women from all social classes were now actively involved in the struggle for women's rights. Women workers, who had been reluctant to organize since the beginning of the industrial revolution, realized that trade unionism was an indispensable tool.

It is impossible in this book that focuses on the feminist movement to describe all the stages of the women's labour movement. Suffice it to say that many exceptional women were active in the unions that emerged during the period. When 4,000 women garment workers went out on strike in Montréal in 1934 and again in 1937, Léa Roback was one of their leaders. She decried the unjust conditions to which women workers were subjected just because they were women: sexual harassment by foremen, lack of women's washrooms, lack of maternity leave, unequal pay, and unhealthy working environments. She also helped pregnant

Léa Roback (1903-2000) was a feminist activist, union organizer and leader in the Voice of Women.

workers obtain illegal abortions. When the Church persisted in its tight control of all women's organizations, Léa Roback shouted, "Prayers don't build a union!"

Even the nurses organized to improve their working conditions. What, striking nurses? Impossible! Cardinal Villeneuve declared in 1936, "Nurses do not have the right, in all conscience, to place their immediate material advantages before their moral and spiritual obligations, compared to which nothing else is more important."

The Ligue des droits de la femme and the Alliance canadienne pour le vote des femmes du Québec were also interested in the situation of women workers. They denounced the labour legislation as inadequate, decried the absence of women on the minimum wage commission, and called for a national inquiry on the situation of women workers. Meanwhile, many lawmakers claimed that working women were responsible for the economic crisis. This was ironic, given that it was ordinary women, homemakers, who enabled the

In the 1930s feminist "sandwich women" walked through the streets wearing posters for women's suffrage. The English posters used the words *justice* and *equality*, but these words did not appear on the French posters.

population to survive during the Depression.

Feminists were also scandalized by the exploitation of female teachers, who earned only $150 per year, sometimes as low as $80 annually. This translated into a weekly salary of $2 or $5, even less than a female factory worker earned. In a radio talk, Thérèse Casgrain exclaimed about the salary of women teachers, "A female labourer would never accept this pittance."

Since taking a public stand did not have much impact on the daily reality of women workers, obtaining the provincial vote became more important than ever. This was also the opinion of Laure Gaudreault, a teacher in the Charlevoix region. She affirmed,

"These government men think that by improving municipal budgets they will calm down the voters. But the woman teacher, who is not entitled to vote, has nothing to lose." In 1937, Laure Gaudreault succeeded in unionizing rural teachers, women who were willing to teach in country schools where working conditions were the most arduous.

In 1937, after many years of pressure, the government passed the *Needy Mothers Assistance Act*. Late in coming and limited in scope, it made assistance subject to mothers meeting moral and religious criteria. Thousands of mothers were excluded from assistance, especially "unwed mothers," as they were known back then. They were forced to leave their children in orphanages, as did many poor families who had no other choice. After ten years of the Depression, the orphanages were bursting at the seams.

ACTIONS TO PROMOTE THE RIGHT TO VOTE

During this desperate time of economic crisis, feminists continued to promote women's provincial voting rights in Québec. In 1929, Idola Saint-Jean published a bilingual column in the *Montreal Herald*. She described how economic circumstances for women had improved in the provinces where they had won the right to vote. Her column generated masses of letters, most of them favourable to her ideas.

In 1930, two women ran in the federal election: Dr. Grace Richie-England for the Liberal Party in Mont-Royal, and Idola Saint-Jean in Dorion-Saint Denis as an independent. They were not elected, but they did make an impact, despite all the criticism. Idola Saint-Jean got 3,000 votes. The candidates used the election as an opportunity to publicize their arguments for women's suffrage.

In 1931, the Société Saint-Jean-Baptiste chose the theme of "Women in Québec History" for its annual Saint-Jean parade held every year on June 24 to celebrate Québec and the Québécois. One of the floats would represent women of the early 19th century, when women had the right to vote. Idola Saint-Jean immediately offered to sponsor it on behalf of the Alliance canadienne pour le vote des femmes du Québec. The Société Saint-Jean-Baptiste refused the offer, saying that the parade must not provoke controversy. Anti-feminism was never far from the surface in nationalist circles.

Idola Saint-Jean founded a yearly magazine in 1933, *La Sphère féminine*, in which she defended the goals of the feminist movement. Feminists also made use of a new medium: the radio. From 1933 to 1938, the weekly radio program, *Fémina*, hosted by Thérèse Casgrain and Florence Fernet-Martel, explained the significance of the vote to women listeners and informed them about the different forms of injustice to which women were subjected. Like Idola Saint-Jean's newspaper column, this radio show generated masses of correspondence. Feminists had won the support of several progressive figures. Every week in *Le Monde ouvrier*, a writer named Julien Saint-Michel published a front-page article that frequently supported feminist demands. Who was Julien Saint-Michel? It turned out that Julien was the pseudonym of Éva Circé-Côté, a woman journalist. With a male pseudonym, she was free to write about controversial subject matters.

Feminists organized lectures and published articles in magazines such as *La Revue populaire* and *La Revue moderne*; they walked the streets wearing sandwich boards bearing slogans. On the occasion of the Royal Jubilee in 1935, they presented King George V of England with a women's suffrage petition containing 10,000 signatures. In 1937, the Ligue des droits de la femme set up a polling booth at a trade fair. Visitors were asked to vote on women's suffrage. When the results of this improvised survey were announced, there were 8,149 votes for women's suffrage and only 249 against. Attitudes had clearly changed, both in the cities and in the rural areas. Here is a comment from a woman in Saguenay sometime in the 1930s: "I respect my husband's ideas and political convictions, but I absolutely defend the right to hold my own opinions."

In 1937, the federal government established a Royal Commission of Inquiry on Dominion-Provincial Relations to examine the Canadian economy and federal-provincial relations. Several feminist associations presented briefs, including the Ligue des droits de la femme. Their spokeswoman was Elizabeth Monk, a McGill University law graduate who was not entitled to practice law because of her sex. She presented a well-documented brief, much admired by the commissioners, which illustrated the deplorable and discriminatory conditions of women in Québec: inferior pay of women workers and teachers, unemployment insurance regulations that excluded vast numbers of women workers, horrifying statistics on infant mortality, and the exclusion of women from the practice of law.

In 1935, the Ministry of Agriculture once again encouraged the Cercles de fermières movement, which had faltered since 1931 due to the economic crisis. Its agents distributed spinning wheels and looms; classes were organized for rural women, who soon realized they could improve their lot through handicrafts. In 1935, there were 273 circles with 11,800 members. A new magazine appeared, addressed to rural women: *Paysana*. The editor-in-chief, Françoise Gaudet-Smet, had no interest, however, in encouraging women to demand the vote: "A good-hearted woman will better her country by raising her children and performing her role of inspiring others and generating energy." Convinced that they were exercising a "profession," she demanded better working conditions for rural women. But, her readers were more interested in the embroidery, weaving and knitting patterns in the magazine and in the craft fairs being held throughout the province. The number of circles began to increase rapidly. In early 1940, they numbered 718, with a membership of over 40,000 "farm wives." This was substantial, much larger than feminist groups. The Ligue des droits de la femme, for instance, had only 50 odd members and the Alliance, roughly 200. Anti-feminist forces had succeeded in considerably reducing their ranks.

How would such a depleted group of feminists advance the struggle for women's suffrage?

CHAPTER 12

A Winning Strategy

AFTER A DOZEN FRUITLESS pilgrimages to Québec City, feminists were fed up. Thérèse Casgrain decided that if they were going to win the vote, they needed to change their strategy. She was now vice-president of the *Club des femmes libérales*, a women's political club that had existed since 1928. She convinced the leader of the Liberal opposition in Québec, Adélard Godbout, to invite 40 members of Femmes libérales to the Liberal party convention in May 1938. In exchange, she promised they would work for the party in the next election. By the end of the convention, the delegates had succeeded in getting women's suffrage on the party platform. The 800 Liberal delegates voted unanimously in favour of the motion. Maybe the tide was turning?

Meanwhile, international events were having a local impact again, just as they had in 1914. Beginning in 1933, Hitler and his Nazi party in Germany had launched a policy of aggression against Germany's neighbours. Europe was on high alert. Would there be another war, so soon after the Great War which was to end all wars? After Hitler invaded Poland in 1939, other countries, including Canada, declared war on Germany.

In the province of Québec, this announcement elicited a variety of reactions: enthusiasm because the war would create jobs and bring people out of the Depression; but also fear that the federal government would once again impose conscription. Maurice Duplessis chose this moment to call an election. He hoped that the fear of conscription would encourage voters to bring him back into power. With the support of the federal government, however, the Liberals won the election. Would the new premier, Adélard Godbout, abide by his party platform and give women the right

to vote? He announced it in the Throne Speech, sparking outrage among religious leaders.

Thérèse Casgrain is surrounded by members of the Ligue des droits de la femme. In 1940, when Québec women obtained the right to vote, the members of the Ligue gathered to celebrate their victory.

Cardinal Villeneuve, head of the Church in Québec, had the following warning proclaimed in every parish:

> We are not in favour of female political suffrage:
> Because it goes against family unity and the family hierarchy;
> Because voting exposes women to all the passions and adventures of politics;
> Because it appears to us that, in fact, the vast majority of women do not want it; and
> Because the social, economic, and health reforms that are put forward in support of women's suffrage could just as easily be obtained through the influence of feminine associations outside the political sphere.

This official position made things extremely awkward for Premier Godbout. A wily politician, he answered the Cardinal, saying that he was a man of his word, and having promised women's suffrage, he would have the law passed. But, because he did not wish to disobey the Cardinal, he proposed to resign and have himself replaced as premier by the member for Saint-Hyacinthe, the fiery Télesphore-Damien Bouchard. This politician was an adversary of the Church, anti-clerical, and the bane of the bishops because of his radical ideas.

Choosing between an anti-clerical premier and women's suffrage, the Cardinal apparently decided it was less risky not to oppose women's suffrage. The legislation was passed on April 25, 1940. Women had finally won the vote in Québec!

The Ligue des droits de la femme gathered at once to celebrate the victory. During the meeting, Thérèse Casgrain declared, "Our real work has just begun. The vote is a means, not an end."

The women of Québec never turned back. Feminists had won because they refused to give up, even when everyone seemed against them. According to history books, the Liberal Party gave women the right to vote in Québec—but the history books are wrong. Women obtained the right to vote because they persevered for more than 40 years.

Now that they finally had the vote, what would feminists do next?

FEMINIST CAMPAIGN FOR WOMEN'S VOTING RIGHTS

1913   Founding of the Montreal Suffrage Association

1918   Canadian women obtain the right to vote in federal elections after 36 years of struggle

1922   Founding of the Comité provincial du suffrage and demonstration at the National Assembly of Québec

1922   Marie Gérin-Lajoie goes to Rome for the convention of the International Union of Catholic Women's Leagues

1927   Founding of the Ligue des droits de la femme by Thérèse Casgrain

1927   Founding of the Alliance canadienne pour le vote des femmes du Québec by Idola Saint-Jean

1929   Dorion Commission concerning the civil rights of married women

1940   Victory for Québec women: They obtain the vote from the National Assembly after 40 years of struggle.

INTERLUDE

Young Women in 1940

THE YEAR IS NOW 1940. Let me introduce you to the young women of this time: Jeannine, Denise, Gisèle, Claudette, Monique, Madeleine, Lise, Pierrette, and Louise. They are all 17 years old.

Most of them know nothing of feminists or women's rights. They're allowed to attend school for a longer period, but most parents are much more interested in paying for their sons' higher education and girls often get told, "You don't need a degree to change diapers."

In 1940, education was not free of charge; not even primary school was public. In fact, school attendance was not compulsory until 1943. But public school attendance was becoming more common beyond the primary level, with over 8,000 girls in grade 9 and a little over 1,000 in grade 11. It was already the case, even in 1940, that fewer girls dropped out of school than boys.

Many private schools for girls were established by nuns: nearly 40 "normal schools" [teacher training colleges], as well as many schools for domestic science, and some 60 boarding schools that offered "*Cours Lettres-Sciences*," a private secondary school course for girls. About 9,000 girls were enrolled in these private programs. In addition, there were roughly 20 nursing schools and a dozen *collèges classiques* [colleges with a focus on the humanities], most of them run by the nuns. A small minority of girls were enrolled in university, mainly in professional programs such as physiotherapy, medical technology, library science, translation, social work, dietetics, and *pédagogie familiale* [home economics].

For 20 years, feminists had left the education of girls to the nuns. It was thanks to the nuns that girls were able to get an education. But only a minority of girls from wealthy families had access to these schools, because this education was not free. The government refused to fund the boarding schools, normal schools, and colleges run by the nuns. Only the domestic science schools were government-funded.

The fact that more women were receiving an education would surely help bring about change. Yet, at home, Jeannine, Denise, Gisèle, Claudette, Monique, Madeleine, Lise, Pierrette, and Louise were still responsible for household chores. As in the 19th century, they were still their brothers' servants.

By 1940, paid work had become almost fashionable, even among the upper middle class. Naturally, young women entered the traditional female occupations such as teachers, nurses, secretaries, shop girls, and factory workers. At that time, marriage meant automatic dismissal. In all these jobs, the pay remained ridiculously low, well below that of men.

August 1, 1941. During the Second World War it became common to see women taking on new roles. Young women felt that from now on life would be totally different.

Growing numbers of young women were joining associations affiliated with *Action catholique* (a network of community-based Catholic action groups), like *Jeunesse étudiante catholique* [JEC, Catholic Student Youth]. They even attended Church-sponsored marriage preparation classes; when war was declared, young men rushed into marriage to avoid conscription. As the economy recovered, it was easier for young couples to marry, even if housing was scarce—as indeed it was—on a scale never before seen.

Although women now had the right to vote, in 1940, they hadn't yet had the opportunity to vote in a Québec election. As for their civil rights, these were mostly unchanged. Despite 40 years of campaigning, young women were not any more aware than their grandmothers had been of their inferior legal status. Despite everything, optimism was in the air. When the war ended, life would be great!

CHAPTER 13

Women's Role in the War Effort

DURING THE SECOND WORLD WAR, feminists' attention was drawn to new issues. The economy was bolstered by the war and society was propelled into the modern era. The context was also ripe for the rise of unions. Horrendous working conditions and a wartime wage freeze led to numerous strikes.

As in the First World War, the war effort became the first priority of the country. The presence of women in the work force expanded steadily to meet the enormous needs of the various war industries. Between 1941 and 1942 alone, the number of women in the labour market increased five-fold. All levels of government needed women's help to meet the demands of the wartime effort. Advertising campaigns trumpeted the message: *Ménagères, vous êtes en guerre!* [Homemakers, you're at war!].

Women in Rush Hour on June 14, 1943.

De la poêle à frire jusqu'à la ligne de feu. During the Second World War, governments depended on women to meet the demands of war production. Ads were published in women's magazines to convince them to participate in the war effort.

There was a call to women on the home front to save useful materials such as clothing, metal, paper, meat bones, and cooking fat. *"De la poêle à frire jusqu'à la ligne de feu"* [from the frying pan to the front lines] was the message of a poster encouraging housewives to save fat and bones. Everyone was surprised to learn that these products were used to manufacture nitroglycerine, an essential component for making bombs.

Women were needed: to work in shops, to monitor consumer prices, and to serve on the committees that administered ration coupons. Most products were rationed; families were only entitled to meagre quantities of staples such as butter, sugar, eggs, meat, coffee, and tea. Women were needed: to grow fruit and vegetables, to staff the employment centres to ensure that no industry went

De la **POÊLE À FRIRE** jusqu'à la **LIGNE DE FEU**

GLYCÉRINE POUR ADOLPHE BENITO ET TOJO

Gardez TOUTE LA graisse ET LES OS

Le Canada a besoin et **doit avoir** toutes les graisses de rôtis, tous les morceaux de gras de rebut et tous les os de **toutes** les cuisines du pays.

Avec la graisse, on fait de la glycérine, et avec la glycérine, on fait des explosifs. Les os fournissent de la graisse, ainsi que de la colle pour les industries de guerre.

Ne jetez pas une seule goutte de graisse ayant déjà servi, de graisse de bacon, de graisse de rôti ou de friture, ou tout autre genre. Elles sont instamment requises pour gagner cette guerre.

Passez toutes les graisses au tamis ordinaire dans une boite métallique à grande embouchure. Gardez le gras de rebut (cuit ou cru) et tous les genres d'os, cuits, crus ou secs.

Quand vous en avez une livre ou plus, **portez-la à votre boucher.** Il vous paiera le prix fixé pour la graisse et le gras, **ou bien vous pouvez la remettre au Comité de Récupération Municipal de votre localité.**

Travaillez aux munitions dans votre propre cuisine. Dans 10 livres de graisse, par exemple, il y a assez de force explosive pour tirer 49 obus antiaériens. Travaillez donc tous les jours pour la Victoire pendant toute la durée de la guerre.

DEPARTMENT OF NATIONAL WAR SERVICES
NATIONAL SALVAGE DIVISION

F 437F

short of workers and to be those industry workers.

At the Red Cross, women prepared the packages that were sent to soldiers and prisoners of war; they made bandages and warm clothing. At the Fédération nationale Saint-Jean-Baptiste alone, women volunteers produced over 23,000 knitted garments between 1939 and 1945. The Cercles de fermières, the rural women's organizations, knitted just as many.

When German submarines were spotted in the Gulf of St. Lawrence, women became indispensable as civil defence workers to prevent enemy attacks. Committees were set up to organize this army of women volunteers—active in every sector. When someone was needed to coordinate these committees, it was the presidents of women's associations and feminists to whom people turned. They were essentially the only ones available with experience in the public sphere. Wartime made it commonplace to see women assuming major public responsibilities.

Women were galvanized by the debates surrounding conscription, a repetition of what had happened in 1917, during the First World War. Canadian Prime Minister Mackenzie King had promised not to impose compulsory military service, but in 1942, he held a plebiscite asking Canadians to release him from his promise. This led to a new conscription crisis. Women protested as mothers and as activists. Simonne Monet-Chartrand, a young mother with another baby clearly on the way, raised eyebrows when she spoke out against conscription at a public meeting. Thérèse Casgrain, who for 20 years had led the struggle for women's suffrage, decided to run for Parliament in a 1942 by-election as a way to voice her protest against Ottawa's decision on conscription. Although she did not win, she came a respectable second.

The City of Montréal passed a municipal reform in 1940 that created three categories of city councillor, including the "Class C" councillors, who were appointed rather than elected. This category of councillor represented associations and public bodies. Pressure from all the feminist associations resulted in the appointment of two feminist activists, Lucie Bruneau and Elizabeth Monk, as Class C city councillors, representing feminist associations.

As the war drew to a close, the government began planning for when the economy would return to normal and sought the support of women's associations to carry out this delicate operation. In June 1944, the FNSJB gathered together all the women's and feminist organizations. The meeting was attended by 34 groups: members of the Fédération, the Ligue des droits de la femme, women's war committees, women's unions, the Cercles de fermières, and even the Catholic Action groups. The FNSJB's president, Eva Thibodeau, asserted, "Governing means planning ahead."

The government ordered housewives to recover cooking fat: fat was used in the manufacture of nitroglycerine that was used to make bombs.

Françoise Gaudet-Smet, who was in charge of rural social services, played an important role in this meeting, insisting that rural women be taken into account. After the meeting, delegates sent Premier Godbout a list of their demands: free vocational training for women, equal pay with men, the right of married women to keep their jobs, maternity leave, health protection for women workers, electricity for families in rural areas, and mobile health clinics. The demands were, however, modest. These women still believed that going to work as servants or cleaning women was the ideal solution for all the women who would find themselves out of a job after the war factory closures. Unfortunately, these demands did not go any further because two months later with the election of Maurice Duplessis, there was a new government in charge in Québec. Women's demands were put on the back burner again.

Would more Québec women now become interested in politics?

CHAPTER 14

Political Conflicts for Women

IN THE AUGUST 1944 provincial election, Québec women voted for the first time. There were no polls back then, so there is no way of knowing which party they supported. But the Liberal Party was responsible for passing the law that gave women the vote, and in the 1944 election the Liberals won more votes than the Union Nationale party headed by Maurice Duplessis. It was the division of the electoral map and the presence of a third party, the Bloc Populaire, which brought the Union Nationale into power. It seems that the women's vote did not produce the dreaded cataclysm predicted by all those men who had resisted women's suffrage.

Though male politicians and journalists had stopped opposing women's suffrage, the bishops had not had their last word. Catholic Action groups had been growing in strength since the mid-1930s. Catholic associations united groups in almost every social sector, including unions. Only a very few groups escaped the bishops' control. Among them were the Cercles de fermières, the rural women farmers groups attached to the Ministry of Agriculture.

In December 1945, the bishops issued a directive urging the Cercles de fermières to leave their groups and join the *Union catholique des fermières* [Catholic Union of Farm Women], which was supposed to be the women's branch of the *Union catholique des cultivateurs* [Catholic Farmers' Union]. Among the religious authorities' arguments for wanting to bring these farm women back into the Catholic fold was the threat of governmental control over these women's opinions and votes.

"Since women have been favoured with the right to vote," explained one priest, "the fact they belong to these Cercles that

are tied to the State carries with it the possibility that a government with its back against the wall or unscrupulous politicians might be tempted to take advantage of the situation by unduly influencing their votes."

Women were very surprised by this directive. The members of the Cercles de fermières found themselves in the middle of a political quarrel they had never imagined. Some of the Cercles complied with the directive. But surprisingly, nearly 30,000 women took the risk of disobeying the bishops, affirming that economic matters were not the business of the Church. These women wished to continue benefitting from the

Thérèse Forget-Casgrain (1896-1981), pictured at the beginning of her feminist career on page 52, founded the Ligue des droits de la femme in 1928 and gave radio talks in the mid 1930s. She convinced the Liberal Party of Québec to put women's suffrage on its election platform in 1938.

professional assistance of visiting technicians and the agriculture ministry's financial support. Apparently, membership in the Cercles had helped them to develop a higher critical sense and some political savvy.

During this period, a new issue drew feminists' attention: the family allowance. The Canadian government launched a social protection program in which monthly cheques would be sent to mothers to help them financially in raising their children. But in Québec, under the province's civil law, cheques would be sent to the fathers instead. The law could not contemplate two "heads" of the Québec family. Feminists opposed this decision with Thérèse Casgrain and Florence Fernet-Martel leading the protest, supported by several women journalists. Thérèse Casgrain met with the federal Minister of Justice, Louis Saint-Laurent, but was unable to convince him. His reply: "Madam, if this is your view, campaign for what you think is best."

Thérèse Casgrain was indignant: "So that's how it is. Women in the rest of the country have it given to them on a silver platter, but in Québec we have to organize a campaign."

And Thérèse Casgrain proceeded to organize a campaign against *chèques adressés au père* [cheques in the names of the fathers]. She reminded everyone that the *Family Allowances Act* was a federal law, and that it should not be subjected to the *Civil Code of Québec*. Women sent telegrams to Ottawa and spoke on the radio. Québec's political parties, legal authorities, and religious officials were adamant. They believed that a cheque made out to mothers would break up the French Canadian family by eliminating women's financial dependency on their husbands.

Finally, feminists discovered a legal argument. An article of the *Civil Code* stated that a married woman held a *mandat tacite de la gestion du quotidien familial* [tacit mandate to manage the household]. Women asserted that this article entitled mothers to receive the family allowance cheque in their own names. Feminists won the battle and Québec women finally received their first cheque—although a few weeks late, because the cheques had already been printed in the names of the fathers and had to be reissued. For thousands of women, this cheque was the first money they had ever received in their own name. And this they owed to the feminists.

The Bloc Populaire party proposed to boycott these cheques, on the basis of provincial autonomy and paternal authority. The members of the newly formed Union catholique des fermières, among others, were urged to return their cheques. This protest movement was short-lived when the women of Québec cashed their baby bonuses.

Thérèse Casgrain was very familiar with the message underlying the family allowance episode. Since Québec women were at the mercy of the *Civil Code of Québec*, she went to Premier Maurice Duplessis in 1945, to urge him to respond to feminists' longstanding demands concerning married women's legal rights. It was time to resume a battle that had been initiated by Marie Gérin-Lajoie in 1903, when she published a book, *Traité de droit usuel*, in which she argued against the legal subordination of married women. She and other feminists testified before a commission of inquiry in 1929, the Dorion Commission, but had made only the most meagre of gains. The situation had now become intolerable. The question of the civil rights of married women had to be settled, once and for all. The government's response to these urgent claims was to set up yet another commission, the Méthot Commission.

Feminist organizations immediately leapt into action. Unfortunately, two leading activists of the first half of the century were no longer among them; Marie Gérin-Lajoie and Idola Saint-Jean had died in 1945. Women set up a joint committee, made up of the leaders of the principal feminist associations: the Ligue des droits de la femme, the FNSJB, the Association pour l'avancement familial et social [Association for Family and Social Advancement], the Montreal Local of the Council of Women, and the Civics League. The joint committee prepared a brief of far-reaching importance, primarily the work of Elizabeth Monk and Jacques Perreault, a lawyer sympathetic to the cause. The brief argued that since women's economic and social situation had changed, the *Civil Code* should be amended to reflect this new reality.

Women had finally been permitted to practise law in 1941 and in 1946 several women lawyers formed a committee to try to speed up the process of legal reform. In 1947, Marie Gérin-Lajoie's sister, Thaïs Lacoste-Frémont, led the Québec City chapter of the FNSJB in organizing a popular series of classes and lectures on women's civil rights. Many members of the Cercles de fermières and the brand new *Association des femmes de carrière du Québec métropolitain* [Association of Professional Women of Québec], founded in 1947, took part in these activities. In Montréal, Thérèse Casgrain decided to reach out to the Catholic action groups, and together they formed a women's committee to study the question of married women's civil rights. The ideas of Marie Gérin-Lajoie were central to these discussions. Women remembered that this was the reason she had become a feminist at the end of the 19th century. The articles of Marie Gérin-Lajoie, still relevant, were now being studied by a younger generation of women.

Opponents to women's civil rights were numerous. Albert Leblanc, a notary from Sherbrooke, described the women's demands as "a legal absurdity." He huffed: "The *Civil Code* is an incomparable monument to human wisdom and its content is nearly perfect."

Once more, feminists came up against a brick wall. Commissioner Méthot recommended that yet another committee be formed and the legal reforms were postponed pending further review. Throughout the 1950s, discussions on the matter failed to reach a conclusion. In 1954, one decision was finally made: to abolish the infamous article of the *Civil Code* that stipulated a double standard regarding the use of adultery as grounds for separation. Under this provision, a man could separate from his wife if she committed adultery, but a woman could not use adultery as grounds for separation unless her husband brought his mistress into the family home. The amendment eliminating the most archaic part of the *Civil Code* was intended to silence the feminist critics.

Would a new issue succeed in mobilizing feminists?

CHAPTER 15

Where Are the 1950s Feminists?

IN THE 1950s, women continued to fight for the cause of women's equality. But for a period of about 15 years (1945-1960), they were no longer fighting in the name of feminism.

Many women, including women journalists, claimed, "If they are unequal, women only have themselves to blame." Such women believed that since the doors were now open to them, women should shake off the "victim" mentality. Women preferred to work with men in mixed political, trade union, and social organizations, rather than in women-only groups. In 1948, half of the signatories to the artists' revolutionary manifesto entitled *Refus global* [blanket refusal] were women signalling, at least to some, that women had now "assumed their rightful place" in the arts community.

The Fédération nationale Saint-Jean-Baptiste, having failed to recruit any new members, was no longer active. Idola Saint-Jean's group, the Alliance canadienne pour le vote des femmes du Québec, did not survive the death of its founder and president in 1945. The Ligue des droits de la femme basically ceased operations when its president, Thérèse Casgrain, entered formal politics. Between 1942 and 1963, she was a candidate in nine federal and provincial elections for the left-wing Cooperative Commonwealth Federation (CCF), the forerunner of the NDP, though she was never elected. Only the Montreal Local Council of Women remained active after 1950, but it maintained almost no contact with French-speaking women. This group still exists in 2012.

Despite this dramatic decline in participation in feminist organizations, more women than ever before became actively involved in organizations in the 1950s. But, in keeping with the times, these were "mixed" groups (women and men) and women's associations that were not primarily concerned with the status of women. The women who joined these organizations were mainly housewives, although some were professional women, such as journalists, social workers, lawyers, and psychologists.

A review of organizations of the 1950s offers a sampling of women's intense participation in political and social life during that period. Girls joined the Catholic Guides, and Catholic associations such as the *Jeunesse étudiante catholique* [JEC, students], the *Jeunesse ouvrière catholique* [JOC, workers], the *Jeunesse agricole catholique* [JAC, rural youth] and the *Jeunesse indépendante catholique*, [JIC, young office workers of both sexes]. Adult women belonged to several different associations: the *École des parents* [the School for Parents, founded in 1939 and expanded considerably after the war], the *Ligue ouvrière catholique* [Catholic Workers' League, 1939], the *Service de préparation au mariage* [Marriage Preparation Service, 1944], the *Association des femmes de carrière du Québec métropolitain* [Association of Professional Women of Québec, 1947], the *Association canadienne des consommateurs* [Consumers' Association of Canada, 1947], the *Fédération des femmes libérales de la province de Québec* [formerly known as "Club Wilfrid Laurier," the Québec version of the Women's Committee of the Liberal Party of Canada, 1948], the *Fédération des femmes libérales* [Women's Committee of the Liberal Party of Québec, 1950], the *Cercle des femmes journalistes* [Circle of Women Journalists, 1951], the *Cercles d'économie domestique* [Home Economics Circles, 1952], the *Foyers Notre-Dame* [Notre-Dame Homes, 1954], Serena [a birth control service, 1955], the *Association des femmes chefs d'entreprise* [Association of Women Entrepreneurs, 1956], and the *Union catholique des femmes rurales* [the new name of the Union catholique des fermières, 1958]. Only a handful of these groups was not affiliated with the Church.

Of the women's organizations that had been established in the first half of the 20th century, only the Cercles de fermières remained active. Most convent school alumnae clubs, whose federation had dissolved in 1934, had been transformed into social circles that organized card games and reunions. By the 1950s, the Ligue féminine catholique, which had been formed in 1929, was attracting only older women.

Only two newly formed organizations in the 1950s pursued explicitly feminist goals. The *Association des femmes universitaires*, founded in 1949 by Florence Fernet-Martel, fought for girls' access to higher learning. They organized information meetings and offered a scholarship.

Florence Fernet-Martel (1894-1986) worked tirelessly as Secretary of La Ligue pour les droits de la femme to obtain the right to vote for women in Québec. She was a co-founder of the Association des femmes universitaires [the University Women's Club] of Montréal.

The *Ligue des femmes du Québec*, founded in 1957 by several women trade unionists, was concerned with the working conditions of women workers and they presented briefs on women's civil rights. They also demanded that all women have the right to vote in municipal elections. However, these two groups had only 40 or 50 members and were relatively unknown.

Young women were adopting modern styles of dress—wearing pants, shorts, sleeveless dresses and sundresses. And with this new approach to fashion, the bishops lost their battle for female modesty. The arrival of television in 1952 brought about important changes. Television, much more than radio, introduced new ideas into every sector of society and transformed people's lives. For the first time, women were public figures, serving as new role models for young women. With her popular TV show *Toi et moi* [You and Me], running from 1954 until 1960, Janette Bertrand helped raise women's awareness about the problems of modern couples. She also wrote an advice column in *Le Petit Journal*, a paper popular among working class women.

HIGHER EDUCATION FOR YOUNG WOMEN

The education of women was a hot topic. Between 1947 and 1953, a public debate raged. On one side were those who advocated a traditional education for girls, provided by the domestic science schools popularly known as the *écoles du bonheur* ["happiness" schools]. On the other side were the proponents of serious higher learning for girls. Many women expressed their views in public talks and articles in newspapers and magazines. The first woman in Québec to hold a doctorate in psychology, Monique Béchard, became the champion of a classical humanities education for girls. She challenged the popular disparaging attitude toward "bluestockings" (as women who pursued higher education were called), the practice of separating education based on sex, and the unfairness of depriving girls of genuine intellectual training. She also supported the plight of single women and contradicted the commonly held assumption that all women were expected to have children.

At the end of the 1950s, as increasing numbers of young women were enrolling in higher education programs and earning bachelor's degrees, academic authorities tried to impose a bachelor's program for women only that was different from the one for young men. This time, it was the nuns who protested that men's colleges had been publicly subsidized since 1922, while women's colleges had received no public funding. The nuns were also determined that their female students be allowed to practise any profession they chose. As one nun said in 1958, "We don't have to ask ourselves if a woman should work or not. Women's labour is a fact; it is even a right." She added, "It is unjust to prevent a woman from practising a profession, or to allow her to do only those jobs that require less education, [those jobs that] are less remunerated and less influential."

FROM THE PERSPECTIVE OF WOMEN WORKERS

Paid work for women had been a major concern since the end of the war. Social worker Gabrielle Carrière published *Comment gagner sa vie* [How to Earn a Living] in 1942. It was a bestseller, often given to young women as a graduation present. Her messages were clear. Women can apply for almost any job. Fathers are wrong to oppose their daughters' employment on the assumption that they will eventually marry. Employment is a right and enables single women to support themselves. To those who disagreed, her reply was, "If we do not want young women to work, it is only fair that single men who earn a salary be compelled to marry."

Although attitudes were changing, there was still much disapproval of women with children who went to work, especially mothers of young children. Many women did not tell their employer that they were getting married in order to keep their jobs. Yet thousands of married women and mothers in the working class and in the agricultural sector had been working in the paid labour force for some time. It seemed no one had noticed.

Once they were in the paid labour force women's participation in labour unions became an issue. After opposing unions for a long time, the Catholic Church finally came around to accepting the idea of unions. It created Catholic unions that in 1921 were organized into a large federation of trade unions, called the *Confédération des travailleurs catholiques du Canada* (CTCC), later known in English as the Confederation of National Trade Unions (CNTU). Since its inception, the attitude of this labour federation had been clear. Women belong in the home. Labour unions had always been opposed to the presence of women in the paid work force, especially married women.

Because so many more women were entering the workforce, the CTCC finally relented by forming a women's committee in 1952. But this *Comité féminin* [Women's Committee] focussed mostly on issues concerning the wives of workers, women's role in the family, and whether women even had the right to work. Its leader, Jeanne Duval, eventually became vice-president of the CTCC. Huguette Plamondon, another Québec union activist, became the Vice-President of the Canadian Labour Congress. In both labour organizations, however, it was still very difficult to convince women to take part in union activities, which were still overwhelmingly dominated by men.

Teachers began to unionize in the early 1940s, following the example of the rural women's teachers union founded by Laure Gaudreault in 1937. In 1946, when all the teachers' unions merged into the *Corporation des instituteurs catholiques* [Catholic Teachers Association, CIC] rural women teachers found themselves under-represented in the new organization, even though they made up over 70 per cent of the membership. Their objectives were eclipsed by those of the male teachers. They even lost their newsletter, *La Petite Feuille*. It was still unacceptable for a woman teacher, although more experienced and more competent, to earn more than a young male teacher. Male teachers who married automatically obtained a wage increase; woman teachers who married were fired. Although Laure Gaudreault was elected vice-president of the CIC, women teachers still failed to make any gains. The principle of "equal pay for equal work" was a long way from being accepted in this union.

Historic strikes broke out in many different sectors and a few women trade unionists played a key role, in particular Léa Roback and Madeleine Parent. It is important to note that the type of unionization being offered to women in the 1950s contrasted markedly with the women's trade unionism earlier imagined by Marie Gérin-Lajoie for women workers in the Fédération nationale Saint-Jean-Baptiste. Whereas at the start of the century women workers had focussed on mutual aid and individual training, now the focus was on working conditions and wages. Strikes were now regarded as a legitimate course of action.

Still, in the 1950s, while the number of women entering the paid workforce continued to increase, public opinion continued to hold that a woman's place was in the home. This traditional attitude was reflected in the media, with full-page magazine ads glorifying the *reine du foyer*, the "happy homemaker." In that decade, every young girl's dream was to get married, have a family, and own a pretty little house in the suburbs. Since women's wages remained ridiculously low and women were confined to jobs that were less respected, as well as less valued, it was not surprising that young women wanted marriage and family life more than anything else.

This is why family associations became so popular during the 1950s. And it is also why women began to take an interest in birth control. No longer did they want to raise masses of children as their mothers had done.

DISCONTENT

In 1961, Montréal's Société Saint-Jean-Baptiste once again chose the very traditional image of "woman as the mother of the nation" as the theme for the St-Jean parade. They called it *Hommage à la femme canadienne-française* [Tribute to the French Canadian Woman]. In honour of the occasion, the Montréal daily *Le Devoir* published a special section in which dozens of notable women, including many journalists, put forward their ideas about a new generation of socially engaged women. With the exception of Thérèse Casgrain, all the women quoted below were prominent journalists of the time.

"Women should either withdraw or take on the fight," commented Renée Geoffroy.

"Being a woman is not a profession or a social status," affirmed Adèle Lauzon.

"We must categorically refuse to be shunted into female occupations," declared Solange Chaput-Rolland.

"Girls today can see that freedom and equality do not exist," commented Andréanne Lafond.

"It is up to the more realistic and less romantic young women of today to break the vicious cycle," predicted Judith Jasmin.

"How long," asked Thérèse Casgrain, "will women wait before fully assuming their role in building the nation? Before they claim and hold the positions of authority that are rightfully theirs?"

"I wonder whether French Canadian women are as happy in their homes as everyone thinks," pondered Jeanne Sauvé.

All these comments spoke of discontent among enterprising women. It was the "problem that had no name." At the same time, another journalist, Germaine Bernier, declared, "The wind of human promotion has torn the banners of yesteryear's suffragettes. Activist feminism must give way to something else."

Women were now faced with a contradictory message: The time of feminist demands was over, but women's situation was still far from satisfactory.

Was feminism on the way out?

CHAPTER 16

Women and "their" Quiet Revolution

THE BEGINNING OF the 1960s signalled Québec's arrival into the modern age. Women were active members of all the political, cultural, and social organizations of the time: groups such as Action de la jeunesse canadienne [Canadian Youth Action], the Mouvement laïque de langue française [French-language Secular Movement], the Rassemblement pour l'indépendance nationale [Assembly for National Independence, known by its French abbreviation RIN] and many others. These activists did not discuss their situation as women. In 1966, the CTCC's women's committee ceased to exist. They announced their demise with a press release stating: "Any committee composed solely of women will convince the female union member that she is not really a part of the trade union movement."

Yet women knew that since 1940 they had been full citizens under the law and they were determined to act on their hard fought status. While a series of political and cultural changes were unfolding in Québec, women, too, were experiencing their own Quiet Revolution.

LEGAL RIGHTS OF MARRIED WOMEN

The most urgent matter in the 1950s was the legal status of married women. Feminists in Québec had been campaigning on this issue since the end of the 19th century. Florence Fernet-Martel, a member of the Fédération des femmes libérales, took up the strategy used by Thérèse Casgrain in 1938 in the struggle to win the vote. In 1959, she convinced members of the Liberal Party to include *Civil Code* reform in their party platform. When the Liberals took power in 1960, women expected the law to change. But the result was predictable:

Marianna Jodoin (1881-1980) was the leader of the Fédération des femmes libérales. In 1953, she was the first Francophone woman and the first woman from Québec to be appointed to the Senate.

the issue stalled. The committees that were supposed to draft the new law took their time coming up with proposals.

"Are women going to have to do it ourselves?" protested Réjane Laberge-Colas, a lawyer who later became the first president of the Fédération des femmes du Québec.

POLITICAL EDUCATION

The leaders of the *Fédération des femmes libérales* wanted to provide political training to their 20,000 members. Until then, women in the party had mostly worked on fundraising (banquets, etc.) and taking care of social relations. One of the Fédération's most dynamic presidents, Marianna Jodoin, who went to Ottawa in 1953 to serve as a senator, decided to turn the Fédération into a political training school. She organized conferences with distinguished speakers and educational opportunities to inform members about party policies. The women who followed Marianna as president planned conferences, set up a political committee, and established training

Thérèse Casgrain (2nd from left) and Simonne Monet-Chartrand (2nd from right) represented the Voice of Women in 1965, with the Canadian Secretary of State for External Affairs, Paul Martin. They were demanding that the government take a stand against nuclear arms.

workshops to familiarize women with parliamentary procedures. They also organized women's political education activities, just as Marie Gérin-Lajoie had done from 1921 to 1927. Liberal party sympathizers in the ridings would now have to take women's opinions into account.

VOICE OF WOMEN

Women were clearly showing their interest in politics. By 1960, they were concerned about the nuclear threat. With the construction of the Berlin Wall in 1961 and the Cuban Missile Crisis in 1962, the Cold War was raging and the international situation seemed dire.

In July 1960, a pacifist group called the Voice of Women was formed in Toronto. It united women who opposed the use of nuclear weapons. Branches began to open up across Canada. In early 1961, Thérèse Casgrain created the Québec branch, the *Voix des femmes*, and shortly afterward, became president of the Canada-wide group. Working with Thérèse Casgrain were women leaders such as Marianna Jodoin, Ghislaine Laurendeau, Simonne Monet-Chartrand, Léa Roback, and Solange Chaput-Rolland. More than 500 women joined the Voix des femmes. It engaged in many activities:

national conventions, a fundraising campaign for the Canadian Institute of Peace Research, international meetings in Geneva and Vienna, picketing in Washington, D.C., a delegation on the Peace Train to Ottawa, and the organization of an international meeting in Saint-Donat, north of Montréal, where the journalist Judith Jasmin made a stirring speech. They even made a controversial trip to the other side of the Iron Curtain to an international conference in Moscow. Voix des femmes activists closely monitored the election campaigns in 1962 and 1963, questioning candidates about their positions on the nuclear threat.

Women in Québec mobilized for peace and expressed their solidarity with women around the world. A young woman named Lucile Durand made a revolutionary proposal in the magazine *Cité libre*. Stop making babies, she ordered, because "if we are consistent with our own principles, honest people should stop procreating until we have total disarmament." The emergence of Voix des femmes was living proof that international politics had become a major concern of women in Québec.

Claire Kirkland was the first woman to be elected to the Québec Parliament in 1961. In 1962, she was appointed Minister without portfolio. Later she became Minister of Transportation (1964-1966), Tourism, Game and Fishing (1970-1972) and Cultural Affairs (1972-1973). Among her many responsibilities, she championed Bill 16, which eliminated the subordination of married women in 1964, and the legislation that created the Conseil du statut de la femme in 1973. In this 1971 photo, she is addressing a group of men in her role as Minister of Tourism. To her right is the Mayor of Montréal, Jean Drapeau.

HATLESS WOMAN ELECTED TO GOVERNMENT

In a by-election in December 1961, a woman named Claire Kirkland was elected to the National Assembly—a first for Québec. Later, she would become minister in a number of high profile portfolios.

An old parliamentary rule prohibited women from entering the National Assembly without a hat. This is why feminists of the 1930s always wore hats when they made their annual pilgrimage to Québec City to hear parliamentarians discuss women's suffrage. Claire Kirkland firmly opposed this rule and refused to work in a hat. A daily newspaper in Québec City reported on the new MNA: "A hatless woman in the National Assembly!" In the end, she won.

Women hoped that at last, now that a woman was in the Québec legislature, the law to change the legal status of married women would be passed more quickly. After all, the proposal had been part of the Liberal Party platform since 1958. But not so fast.

TWO WOMEN NAMED TO PARENT COMMISSION

In the early 1960s, the Québec government formed a royal commission on education, called the Parent Commission. Two women were appointed to sit on this Commission: Sister Laurent-de-Rome, a nun from the Congregation of Sainte-Croix who taught philosophy in a women's college, and Jeanne Lapointe, a professor of literature at Université Laval. These two women would ensure that all girls would be able to attend the new schools.

"My goal," said Commissioner Arthur Tremblay, "is to ensure that no boy in Québec is prevented from pursuing the education he chooses."

"And no girl either, I hope!" interjected Jeanne Lapointe.

"Have you turned into a feminist?" asked Gérard Filion, another commissioner.

Clearly, the commissioners considered the idea of girls having access to all levels of education as an essentially feminist proposition. Many women's organizations presented briefs, among them the *Association des femmes diplômées des universités* [the Québec branch of the Canadian Federation of University Women, the new name of Femmes universitaires].

WOMEN READING A REVOLUTION

In 1960, a new French Canadian women's magazine hit the newsstands: *Châtelaine*. It advertised itself as a determined new voice for women. Its editor-in-chief, Fernande Saint-Martin, was decidedly "feminist" in her language. Each of her editorials urged women to think for themselves and take action. In 1962, she urged women to organize and make their demands heard: "Women unite."

Amid the fashion photos, recipes, and make-up tips, *Châtelaine*'s readers discovered progressive new thinking. There were articles on free education, birth control, changes to the *Civil Code*, and women's work lives. The magazine was hugely popular, attracting over 100,000 readers with the first issue.

In 1963, another publication stunned housewives in North America. This time it was in English. *The Feminine Mystique* by the U.S. writer, Betty Friedan, caused a sensation. It was an instant bestseller. Women discussed it in the pages of *Châtelaine* and on TV and it was quickly translated into French. The book named and proposed an explanation for the unhappiness of countless women who were stuck in their homes. Women realized that, to varying degrees, they were victimized by a system that made them think their world should consist only of their families and their homes, and that they should find happiness by making their families happy.

"Did I go to college for this?" asked many educated women, prisoners of domestic routine.

CIVIL RIGHTS FOR WIVES

In 1964, Minister Claire Kirkland finally managed to introduce Bill 16 to the National Assembly, a Bill to abolish the legal subordination of married women by their husbands. Feminists had fought for this since the start of the 20th century. Feminists had presented briefs before commissions of inquiry in 1929 and 1946. The Fédération des femmes libérales had carefully studied the question. Feminists had published dozens of articles on the subject. At last, the legislators gave in. Feminists had waited more than 60 years for this moment.

For the first time in Québec, wives were considered equal to their husbands within the family. They could sign contracts, choose the family residence, work in a field that was different from that of their husband, and act as executors of wills, legal guardians, and tutors. They no longer needed their husband's signature to perform basic acts of civil life. Just think, they could even sign their own lease or take out a bank loan.

Surprisingly, instead of enthusiasm and celebration, Bill 16 was greeted with a flood of criticism, especially from notaries and other law practitioners. Some thought the Bill had not gone far enough. Others protested this attack on male authority in the family. Despite the new law, directors of banks and credit unions and public officials continued to insist on the husband's signature. It would be a long time before mainstream attitudes and practices caught up with the law.

EXPO 67

As early as 1965, the City of Montréal began to prepare for the famous international exhibition of 1967, *Terre des hommes* [Man and his World]. Women journalists were invited to an information session about this major event. Rather than being pleased, as the organizers had intended, these newswomen protested the title, which so clearly evoked the traditional role of women in a "man's world." One journalist noted: "It looks like the major phenomenon of our modern era, the evolution of women, has been forgotten." These critics deplored the secondary role of women in the planning of this world event and the immense female potential being ignored by Expo's directors. And why were women being cast merely as "hostesses"?

This was just another example of the growing dissatisfaction amongst women who realized that their opinions were not being heard. Increasingly, the same question returned: Are we really being treated as equals? It was time to organize again. Just as feminists had organized at the dawn of the 20th century, a critical mass was needed to protest the status quo.

Was feminism poised for a comeback?

CHAPTER 17

Founding of the Fédération des femmes du Québec and AFÉAS

THE YEAR 1965 marked 25 years since Québec women had won the vote. Once again, Thérèse Casgrain stood at the centre of an event, and organized feminism was back on the map. She decided that the anniversary should be celebrated with a conference that would include *all* women—young and old, traditional and modern, urban and rural. Invitations went out to the members of all the women's associations.

The organizers developed a program for the two-day conference entitled *La femme du Québec, Hier et aujourd'hui* [The Woman of Québec, Yesterday and Today]. Claire Kirkland, Québec's first female MNA, was asked to give the opening address. Marianna Jodoin, Québec's first woman senator, served as honorary president. Writer Françoise Loranger created the welcoming introduction in the program, which she entitled "Wake up, sleeping beauty! Wake up!"

The conference became a call for women's freedom and solidarity, and for the right to denounce inequality and the treatment of women as second-class citizens. The 500 attendees discussed legal, economic, and social questions: divorce, daycare, maternity leave, equal pay, access to all the professions, free education, higher learning for girls, women's working conditions, birth control, and legal rights in marriage. It ended with a plenary session moderated by the journalist Lise Payette, a well-known figure with a popular radio show called *Place aux femmes*.

The journalists in attendance promised to give the event unprecedented media coverage. The next day the conference was on the front page of all the newspapers. This was a first—usually news about women was relegated to the "women's page."

Lise Payette was a Québec feminist journalist who hosted the daily radio program *Place aux femmes*, and the television show *Appelez-moi Lise*. She was elected to the Legislative Assembly in 1976, and held a number of cabinet positions in the Parti Québécois government, including the Minister of State for Women, where she led significant reforms in family law.

"The era of recriminations is over. The structures are going to change," read a headline in *Le Devoir*.

"A new image of the Québec woman is taking shape," reported *La Presse*.

"A new strike force" exclaimed Renaude Lapointe, two days later in an editorial in *La Presse*.

Conference participants unanimously supported the recommendation to create a new feminist organization. True to form, that same year Thérèse Casgrain invited a group of women from different backgrounds to her home to prepare a document that would define the framework and operation of the new Fédération. It was to include most of the women's and feminist organizations in Québec.

The founding document for the Fédération was presented the following year. Once again, female journalists were on board, publishing new articles every week. In June 1966, the Fédération des femmes du Québec (FFQ) was born. Most women's groups joined, regardless of their religion, language, or ultimate goals. The FFQ had no ties with religious or political parties. It was to be totally

non-partisan, just like the National Council of Women of Canada had been at the end of the 19th century. The goal was to represent *all* women.

"Won't there be a division of interests between the "women with degrees" and the "women with babies?" asked one female journalist.

"No," answered its first president, Réjane Colas. "When we concern ourselves with a particular class, it will be because their problems affect the whole population."

The Fédération also included individual members, who were themselves members of regional councils. Thus, the FFQ had a presence in Québec City, Montréal, Sherbrooke, Thetford-Mines, and Chicoutimi. The FFQ leadership often came from these geographically diverse regions in Québec.

OTHER WOMEN'S ORGANIZATIONS

Three large groups decided to remain outside the FFQ, even though their members had been part of the discussions at the 1965 conference and again at the 1966 founding conference. The Union

catholique des femmes rurales (1945) and the Cercles d'économie domestique (1952) had just merged into a new association called the *Association féminine d'éducation et d'action sociale* [Women's Association for Education and Social Action] better known by its acronym *AFÉAS*. Its leaders preferred to consolidate their new group before joining the FFQ. The priests who supervised the merger wanted the new association to include "Catholic" in its name, but the women wanted their relationship with the Church to be freely chosen rather than forced.

"The predominant theme is women," affirmed Azilda Marchand. "That is who our members are."

From the start, AFÉAS boasted 35,000 members, mainly wives and mothers. When the merger discussions began, the Cercles de fermières were also invited, since all three organizations shared similar aims. But the Cercles decided against the merger because they would have had to abandon their name and forsake their 50th anniversary celebration. Preferring to maintain their independence, they did not want to join the FFQ either. They wanted to function autonomously from the other women's organizations and resisted the idea of religious neutrality.

Barely on their feet, the two new organizations FFQ and AFÉAS threw themselves into action. They organized political and social action classes and study committees. At the time, few members, even the leaders, identified themselves as feminists, but their aims were those of the preceding generations of feminists. Their goal was to enable women to play an active role in society. At AFÉAS, for example, members educated themselves about the transformation of the education system, social services, and the health care system. Women from remote regions became extremely well informed about the different stages of the Quiet Revolution, often becoming better informed than their husbands.

Women in the new organizations rapidly learned the art of presenting briefs, organizing press conferences, and writing grant proposals. Seeking money was another big step forward for women. Up until that time, activists had almost always done their feminist work as volunteers. Grant money meant that some women could be paid. A series of presidents came and went, committees were formed, and many new responsibilities were shared. There was no shortage of work. Yet during all this activist work, the word "feminist" was barely mentioned—neither in the groups' documentation nor in the newspapers reporting their events.

Meanwhile, these path breakers were frequently aided by television journalists, who initiated opportunities to discuss the burning issues of the day. In 1966, Michelle Lasnier began directing the daily TV show *Femmes d'aujourd'hui* [Women Today], broadcast on Radio-Canada, the French CBC. It was a forum where new ideas were discussed regularly.

Even though these women activists were careful not to call themselves feminists, the opposition was overtly anti-feminist.

According to Solange Chalvin, "women's associations create the illusion that other women are going to solve the problems of every woman."

"Feminism and women's groups undermine women's emancipation," commented a male trade unionist in 1966.

What were the priorities of these new women activists, who no longer dared to call themselves "feminists"?

CHAPTER 18

The Royal Commission on the Status of Women

WHILE THE FFQ and the AFÉAS were holding their founding meetings, women in the rest of Canada were forming similar groups. Members of the pan-Canadian organization Voix des femmes/ Voice of Women met regularly to carry out their collective actions. Women from Québec united with their English-Canadian sisters in the House of Commons in Ottawa concerning a high priority issue for women at that time: birth control. At the end of the 1960s, even after the arrival of the "pill," birth control was still illegal under Canada's *Criminal Code*. The *Criminal Code* also prohibited abortion. Anyone who wanted to provide public information on birth control had to hide their real aim. Even though they were illegal, birth control clinics, known as "family planning clinics," operated openly in Montréal.

Many groups pressured the government to change this obsolete law and women across Canada united around the issue. The founding of the Fédération des femmes du Québec in 1966 galvanized women activists in the rest of Canada, who had just formed the Committee for the Equality of Women in Canada. The two organizations joined forces and lobbied the federal government to create a royal commission on the status of women. Since the early 1960s, similar inquiries had been conducted in many countries, including the U.S., West Germany, France, United Kingdom, Finland, the Netherlands, and Austria. Why couldn't Canada also conduct an in-depth examination of this question?

For once, women's lobbying efforts bore fruit. By the end of 1967, the federal government had set up the Royal Commission on the Status of Women. Among the commissioners were Québec demographer Jacques Henripin and Professor Jeanne Lapointe,

formerly of the Parent Commission. The secretary of this commission was Monique Bégin, a founding member of the FFQ. Presided over by Florence Bird, the Royal Commission on the Status of Women (or the Bird Commission, as it was sometimes called) was an opportunity for all women's groups to consult their members and to prepare briefs that carefully documented the current status of women. Public hearings were held in all the major cities of Canada. Hundreds of women packed into the meeting rooms. The Commission ordered studies on many different questions.

Florence Bird (1908-1998) was a broadcaster and journalist known as Anne Francis. Appointed the Chair of the Royal Commission on the Status of Women (1967-1970), she entered the Senate in 1978.

Aboriginal women spoke out against the *Indian Act* which, since it came into force in the 19th century, had deprived them of their ancestral rights. If an Aboriginal woman married a non-Aboriginal man she lost her Indian status, while a non-Aboriginal woman who married an Aboriginal man gained Indian status. In 1967, Mary Two-Axe Early, a Mohawk woman from Kahnawake, Québec, founded a provincial organization called Equal Rights for Indian Women, the first Aboriginal women's association in Canada. This later became the national organization, Indian Rights for Indian Women.

Mary Two-Axe Early (1911-1996), a Mohawk from Kahnawake in Québec, received the Governor General's Award for the Person's Case in 1979. When she married a non-Aborginal man, she lost her Indian status as a result of section 12(1)(b) of the *Indian Act* and was forced to leave the reserve. She embarked on a campaign to regain her status, creating Equal Rights for Indian Women (later called Indian Rights for Indian Women). The offending section was removed from the *Act* and on July 5, 1985 she was the first woman to be restored to Indian status.

The FFQ and AFÉAS focussed their demands on education: equality for women in all academic programs, special programs for homemakers, vocational training programs. While the FFQ was mainly concerned with women's independence through employment, AFÉAS believed that "we do not need to minimize the contribution to humanity of women in the home and incite women to leave on just any pretext."

The *Alliance des professeurs de Montréal* presented a brief denouncing the stereotypical depictions of women and girls in school textbooks that had the effect of encouraging female students to be passive and assume traditional roles. This was the first time that such an opinion had been expressed in a public forum.

The FFQ took part in the Royal Commission by organizing a major inquiry, *La participation des femmes québécoises à la vie civique* [participation of Québec women in civic life]. The inquiry involved nearly 900 women from all sectors and regions, and collected the opinions of 35 individuals who took part in a series of panel discussions. It was the first time there had been a systematic study of women's opinions about public life. According to FFQ president Rita Cadieux, women should get involved in politics. She declared, "We don't believe that it should be up to women to do the charitable work, while men run the government."

The Royal Commission set off a massive consciousness-raising process. Women's magazines published articles of investigative journalism with details of the history of Québec feminism. People were amazed to discover that Québec women had formulated many more demands than other Canadian women, and that their ideas were sometimes more radical.

The women who were mobilized by the Royal Commission represented a new generation of activists. Their numbers included sociologists, economists, social workers, lawyers, and psychologists. They were doing the "real work" that Thérèse Casgrain had called for in May 1940. Most of the women engaged by the Royal Commission were between 35 and 50 years old. Younger women did not feel particularly involved in what was happening at the government level. Many of them were successfully assuming their rightful place in society. With the advent of free education through vocational schools and junior colleges and a loans and scholarship program, the doors were opened. Young women flooded by the thousands into the new CÉGEPS (free two-year junior colleges from which one could enter university), and universities. Québec had revolutionized the educational system, introducing free education, mixed classes and a myriad of new programs. Young women found ready employment in the expanding sectors of education, health care, and the civil service.

"If I can become a journalist just like a man," opined Lysiane Gagnon, "I don't see why other women can't do the same thing."

"I want to see global social change first and then make changes in male-female relations," explained Louise Harel, then a sociology student and later a leading member of the Parti Québécois.

There was another way to freedom for younger women. Thousands of young women joined the new social and political protest groups that began to appear in the early 1960s. They demanded smoking sections in the teacher training and women's colleges that were still being run by nuns. Expo 67 had opened the world to them. They read eagerly about the political protest movements that were exploding in the United States, France, Germany, Czechoslovakia, and elsewhere. Thousands of women entered into sexual relationships in the permissive environment of the "sexual revolution." Like their male counterparts, they experienced the irresistible sensation of freedom: freedom to travel, freedom to stop attending Mass, freedom to smoke a joint, freedom to listen to their music, and freedom to wear miniskirts. Freedom! Freedom! Freedom!

But would these young women make demands as women?

THEIR RIGHTFUL PLACE, 1940–1969

1945   Campaign to have family allowance cheques
made out to mothers

1946   Resumption of the campaign to obtain civil rights
for married women

1948   Debate about instruction in home economics and
higher education for girls

1950   Founding of Femmes universitaires by
Florence Fernet-Martel

1961   Founding of the Voix des femmes by Thérèse Casgrain

1965   Conference marking the 25th anniversary of Québec
women gaining the vote

1966   Founding of the Fédération des femmes du Québec

1966   Founding of Association féminine d'éducation et d'action
sociale (AFÉAS)

1967   The Royal Commission on the Status of Women

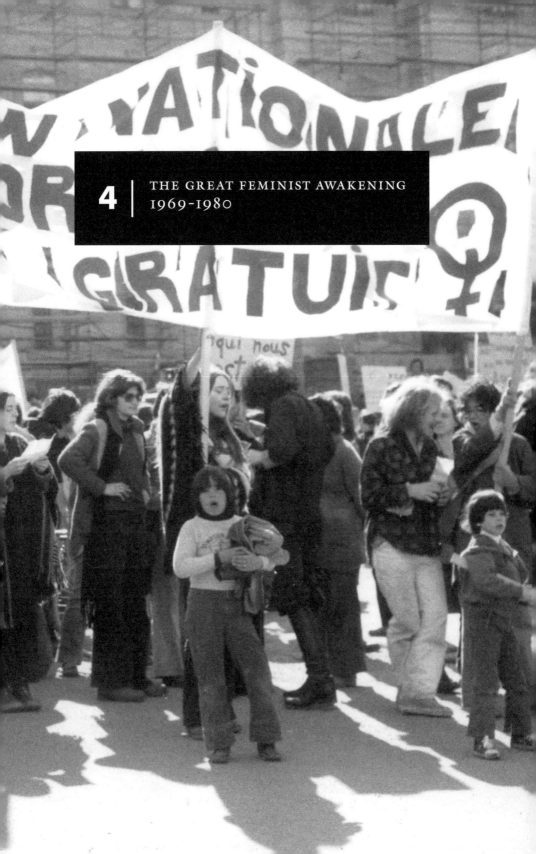

4 | THE GREAT FEMINIST AWAKENING
1969-1980

CHAPTER 19

A New Brand of Feminism

Demonstration in favour of abortion, see p. 130

THE YOUNG WOMEN of the 1970s were not interested nor galvanized by the founding of the Fédération des femmes du Québec. Not in the least, that was for their mothers and aunts. Nationalism and other social and trade union issues were far more compelling.

"Feminism? You mean the suffragettes? Oh, no one is talking about that any more. Francophones are interested in Québec independence and social issues. Women are equal to men now. Feminism? Why do we need it?" said journalist Lysiane Gagnon in 1968. Many women shared her opinion.

Young women supported Québec independence. They attended the meetings of Pierre Bourgault's Rassemblement pour l'indépendance nationale (RIN). They crowded into the now legendary poetry reading, *Nuit de la poésie*. Young women took part in sit-ins at universities and CÉGEPs (the junior colleges). They joined trade unions and political demonstrations in a climate enflamed by the bombs of the Front de Libération du Québec (FLQ), the revolutionary group that blew up targets linked to the federal government.

Young women flocked to the boîtes-à-chanson [coffeehouses] and in 1968, attended the seminal cultural happening, *l'Ostidcho*. Resolutely nationalist, they challenged the language laws by joining mass rallies in front of the National Assembly in Québec City, and protested against Prime Minister Pierre Elliott Trudeau's presence in the reviewing stand at the 1969 Saint-Jean-Baptiste parade in Montréal. They were active in the McGill Français protest of 1969. They attempted to carve a place for themselves in the trade unions. They joined the citizens' committees in working class neighbourhoods and a myriad of social advocacy groups that people were now calling "leftist groups." They proclaimed their solidarity with liberation groups around the world and with the student movement. They travelled to California to connect with activists there. Many young women went to the country to live in communes. Others followed with interest the appearance of Women's Liberation groups in the United States. Young women from McGill University approached several women to talk about creating a Women's Liberation group in Montréal.

In Montréal, in the autumn of 1969, the tension was so high, and trade union, nationalist, and political demonstrations so numerous and militant, that Mayor Jean Drapeau passed a regulation that prohibited public demonstrations, even the Santa Claus Parade. At every demonstration, the police would arrest the men, rarely the women. A group of young women trade unionists and students decided to organize a demonstration against the "anti-demonstration regulation." Now, the police would have to recognize that women were political actors too. Within 48 hours, they succeeded in mobilizing over 250 women to rally at the Monument National on November 29, 1969, coincidentally the very spot where feminists had launched the Fédération nationale Saint-Jean-Baptiste in 1907. But the rally was a political protest, another type of event altogether. The women had barely taken to the streets when the police arrived, systematically arrested everyone, and carried them off to jail. Some women chained themselves together as the English suffragistes had in London at the beginning of the 20th century. The police had to cut their chains in order to bring them to police stations where they were booked, photographed, and finally released on bail.

Next day, the headlines read, "*Le Front commun des Québécoises descend dans la rue.*" [The Québec women's common front hits the streets.]

Two weeks later, a group of these young women met to debrief. Talking together they realized that, although they had been working for social change in many different groups, women's voices were barely heard in those groups. They were angry, and they had seen how powerful the women's demonstration had been. Why not organize for women's liberation?

"When you say that women's oppression exists, everyone laughs at you."

"Or they say [if you are involved in women's liberation] you must have an inferiority complex, or you're a lesbian, or you're sexually frustrated."

"I was really angry when I was at university and in the student movement, because I saw that even in progressive student organizations, men and women were not equal. Women were clearly discriminated against, and could only take lesser roles, like a typist or secretary; we weren't taken seriously."

"In the workers' committee of Saint-Henri, they tried to get women to dance in strip clubs to finance the committee!"

These dissatisfied women decided to start an independent political group for women. They wanted to make waves! Calling themselves the *Front de libération des femmes du Québec*, or FLFQ, they were inspired by the American Women's Liberation movement which protested women's oppression. Defining themselves as *indépendantistes, tiers-mondistes* [third world liberation sympathizers] and *anti-capitalistes*, they were determined to put feminism on the map. Their slogan was: *Pas de libération des femmes sans libération du Québec. Pas de libération du Québec sans libération des femmes.* [No women's liberation without the liberation of Québec. No liberation of Québec without women's liberation.]

They refused to accept the leftist groups' position that Québec independence must be won and capitalism abolished before women's issues could be addressed. They preferred the term "women's oppression" to "status of women" which was a major shift in political emphasis. Their approach was revolutionary and radical, because they wanted to attack the root of this oppression—the patriarchy. Their feminism was anti-patriarchal and anti-capitalist. Their slogan, "the personal is political," reflected their determination to transform, rather than reform, society. Personal relationships mirrored women's inferiority in the public sphere. Why did women have all the responsibility for housework? Why was this work unpaid? Why were women solely responsible for the family?

The FLFQ survived a little over two years and, in 1972, was immediately succeeded by the *Centre des femmes*, which after 1975 gave rise to many new groups. For the next ten years, a new brand of radical feminism espoused by "independent women's groups" (calling themselves "independent" because they refused to permit men to participate in their actions), rocked Québec. And for the first time, the feminists were under 30 years of age.

These radical feminists rejected the usual organizational structures. They ran their groups in a manner totally unlike that of the traditional women's organizations. There were no minutes, no conventions, no chair, no legal incorporation, and no general meetings. Many women insisted on anonymity. They rejected the Fédération des femmes du Québec's approach, labelling FFQ members reformist feminists, women who were simply seeking to integrate into the prevailing system. They, on the contrary, wanted to change the system. They made decisions collectively; everyone had a say; all forms of authority were rejected. Many heated discussions focussed on the political direction and analysis of these new women's groups. Although their lifespan was short, these groups nonetheless managed to turn Québec society upside down.

"Feminists are crazy" many women, including Thérèse Casgrain, muttered.

What directions would these new radical feminists take?

CHAPTER 20

Radical Feminists in Action

BEGINNING IN 1970, Québec feminism separated into several streams. The activists of the Front de libération des femmes du Québec [FLFQ] created "cells," each with a particular mission.

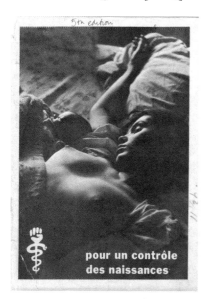

French version of the McGill Birth Control Handbook (February 1970).

Members were united by close emotional ties: When they met, they kissed each other, a new custom in those days. They were accused of being lesbians, the usual charge levelled at feminists. They went out together and took great satisfaction in discovering they could do anything: organize, write, create policy, theorize, all the things that in mixed groups only the men got to do. They took karate classes. They protested the traditional images of femininity by wearing work boots and addressing men openly in the street. They wore no makeup and, while they did not burn their bras, as the media had mythologized, instead they usually went braless. Their actions had a big impact. They were a critical dimension of the impassioned environment of social and political protest of the 1970s.

Abortion was a burning issue. In response to pressure exerted by several groups, the federal government decriminalized birth control and legalized therapeutic abortion on May 14, 1969. The booklet entitled *Pour un contrôle des naissances* appeared in February 1970, the French translation of the *Birth Control Handbook* that had been published by the McGill Student Council in 1968. Some 50,000

FÊTE DES MÈRES
1 jour..... sur 365

La Fête des Mères célèbre la femme épouse et mère

Aujourd'hui choyée et dorlotée,
Demain elle retournera à sa popote et à ses torchons

Pourquoi limiter la vie de la femme à la famille ???

Serons-nous toujours des machines à consommer les
produits de : "General Food" "General Electric"
"Baby's Own" "Wonder-Bra" "Yardley" "Anacin"...

Serons-nous un jour responsable de notre corps et de
notre vie sans attendre que l'homme le soit à
notre place ?

REINE 1 JOUR
ESCLAVE 364 JOURS

NOUS VOULONS ETRE LIBRES

FRONT DE LIBÉRATION
DES FEMMES

The Front de libération des femmes du Québec (FLFQ), founded in late 1969, organized numerous *actions-chocs* [direct actions]. In just a few months, they had totally transformed the feminist movement, without a penny of funding. On May 10, 1970, for Mother's Day, they organized a demonstration in Lafontaine Park to support women's free access to abortion. This is one of the homemade posters waved by women at that rally.

copies were printed and immediately snapped up, necessitating a reprint. Because the booklet talked openly about abortion, it raised the question of where women could obtain one. The Front de libération des femmes set up a new cell, *Avortement*, to manage the referral service the handbook's authors had created in partnership with members of McGill Women's Liberation. They wanted to help women (students, poor women, women from rural areas) who were unable to obtain a therapeutic abortion. The procedure they referred women to cost $250, but no woman was refused if she didn't have the money. They were supported by physicians, notably Dr. Henry Morgentaler, who funded the service and performed the abortions.

The FLFQ created an "X cell" to organize direct actions known as *actions-choc*. On Mother's Day, 1970, they demonstrated in Montréal's Lafontaine Park to denounce this celebration and demand the right to abortion: *Reine un jour, esclave 364 jours!* [Queen for one day, slave for 364 days!] The slogan caught the public's imagination.

The feminist agenda became entwined with the independence movement in Québec. When English Canadian feminists organized the "abortion caravan" to Ottawa, the FLFQ decided not to join them, although they supported abortion. The women said: "We refuse to demonstrate in front of a parliament whose powers over Québec we do not recognize."

In the spring of 1970, Québec was in the midst of an election. Women went to election meetings carrying signs reading, *Mariage = prostitution légalisée*, another bold affirmation of the slogan "the personal is political."

They published a text entitled *Nous nous définissons comme les esclaves des esclaves* [We Define Ourselves as the Slaves of Slaves] and demanded wages for housework, which had never been recognized as real work.

In the autumn of 1970, the Front de Libération du Québec kidnapped Pierre Laporte, the Deputy Premier of Québec, and James Cross, a British diplomat. Laporte was killed and Cross was released after two months in captivity in exchange for safe passage to Cuba. These actions led the federal government to invoke the *War Measures Act* and to make hundreds of arbitrary arrests. This was the famous October Crisis. Although it slowed the pace of the FLFQ's activities, the trial of the *felquistes* [members of the FLQ] in early 1971 was nonetheless an opportunity for a major action. Lise Balcer, a FLQ sympathizer, had been summoned as a witness in one of these trials. She refused to testify because women were not entitled to be jury members in Québec. The judge charged her with contempt of court. Now she, too, was on trial.

When they heard about this, the members of the X cell were furious, and one woman exclaimed, "What? Women don't have the right to be on a jury in Québec?"

They decided to carry out an action at Lise Balcer's trial. With all the media coverage of the trial of the *felquistes*, they would finally succeed in putting feminism on the map. Women occupied the jury box shouting, "Discrimination!" and "The justice system is a hoax!"

The women were charged with contempt of court, convicted on the spot by the judge, without a trial, and sentenced to one month in prison. Two women called out, "They're raping us again!" and their sentence was doubled. All of them were taken directly to

QUEBECOISES
DEBOUTTE !

publié par le centre des femmes
vol. 1, no. 1 - novembre 1972

The Centre des femmes succeeded the FLFQ in 1972. One of its main accomplishments was the continued publication of this radical feminist magazine, launched in November 1971. *Québécoises deboutte* continued publication until March 1973.

Tanguay Prison for Women. Once there, they began working on the rights of women prisoners.

The following July, the law was amended to allow women to serve as jurors. The Fédération des femmes du Québec had been calling for this change for three years. Contempt produced success.

This dramatic episode was followed by other new initiatives. On March 8, 1971, the FLFQ organized the first Québec demonstration to mark International Women's Day. Celebrating IWD began in 1910 by an international conference of socialist women. The FLFQ organized a march in Montréal for free access to abortion, followed by a conference. It was a huge success. The march garnered extensive media coverage and attracted many new members to the group.

In May 1971, the *Lépatatcol* cell [a reference to the potato-based paste used in attaching political posters] burst into the Salon de la femme, a consumer trade fair aimed at women, to denounce the trappings of "femininity" that transformed women into objects: "We don't want your cosmetic culture!" The protesters had hoped to be arrested, but instead they were allowed to carry out their action. Were they being ignored or heeded? The very next year, women's trade fairs included booths devoted to women's health, women's rights, and helping services. Another success.

The FLFQ's next move was to occupy the taverns of Longueuil, a suburb of Montréal, that barred entrance to women. This action received enormous media attention. A short while later these taverns were transformed into brasseries, with a sign at the door that read: "Bienvenue aux dames." Yet another success.

Another FLFQ cell decided to set up a community daycare in 1971, the first women-run daycare centre. At the same time, another cell launched a magazine, *Québécoises deboutte!* [Québec Women Stand Up!] which first appeared in November 1971. Women could finally read articles written in Québec about the revolutionary feminist theory being developed throughout the western world.

Earlier, two activists close to the Front de Libération du Québec had published the *Manifeste des femmes québécoises*, echoing the *Manifeste du FLQ*, which had been published during the October Crisis and which had completely ignored the situation of women. The FLFQ was not directly involved in writing this book, which highlighted the problems of working class women.

All this activity demanded enormous amounts of energy, and it generated tensions. The women who had been jailed disagreed with the others. Some women wanted to focus on reaching ordinary women, sensing that "shock" feminism was scaring them off. Unable to resolve their differences, the FLFQ split in December 1971. Four members of the collective carried on the work of the FLFQ by creating the *Centre des femmes* in January 1972. And the movement continued.

Maintaining the abortion referral service was a priority for the Centre des femmes. After Dr. Morgentaler was arrested on June 1, 1970, the activists at the Centre organized bus trips to New York for women who wanted an abortion. They raised money with grants from the federal government's Local Initiatives Program. In 1972, they collaborated on a book about rape: *Le viol, le crime violent le plus répandu au Québec*. This was a French translation of Susan Griffin's 1971 essay, "Rape: The All-American Crime," with a section about the Québec context. The book sparked massive consciousness-raising among women's groups across Québec.

The taboo against the discussion of violence against women was beginning to crumble. In 1975, feminists in Québec City founded Viol-Secours, a centre where rape victims could get help, information, and legal support. A few months later, the Montréal group *Mouvement contre le viol et l'inceste* opened a similar crisis centre. Other crisis centres sprang up across Québec. Sexual violence against women was another priority issue for radical feminists.

The Centre des femmes' main activity continued to be the publication of *Québécoises deboutte!* The two founders were joined by activists from the Far Left groups that were forming everywhere in Montréal in those days. Their presence provoked endless political debates about the magazine's direction. The leftists accused the founding women of not being totally committed to the Marxist-Leninist line but, in the end, the leftists were excluded. However, this did not prevent the RCMP from raiding the Centre's office twice and confiscating their subscriber list and documentation because of their Far Left connections.

Despite internal strife and external harassment, the Centre managed to continue publishing *Québécoises deboutte!*, producing nine issues between November 1972 and March 1974. The magazine was responding to a genuine need, with over 2,000 subscribers across Québec. It fostered consciousness-raising groups in many regions. Women gathered in these groups to discuss their problems and to use the new feminist analysis to help resolve them. In *Québécoises deboutte!* they read things they had not read anywhere else, except perhaps in the rare book from France or the U.S. The women at the Centre des femmes were committed to their cause. They worked 70-hour weeks, staffing the abortion referral centre, and producing the magazine, including the design, writing, layout, distribution, and instructions to the printer. In addition, they did numerous radio and TV interviews.

But the intensive organizational efforts and ideological discussions became too much of a burden. One activist admitted, "Being in the heat of the action all the time meant we couldn't take time to do the thinking necessary for renewal and creative work." She added: "Most of the activists were haunted by a deep sense of guilt in the face of all the criticisms and could no longer appreciate what the Centre had accomplished." In late 1974, they closed the Centre des femmes. Some of its members continued their feminist activism in new groups that we will learn about in the following chapters.

Would this new brand of feminism replace the Fédération des femmes du Québec?

CHAPTER 21

Fédération des femmes du Québec's Approach:
Lobbies, Briefs, and Conferences

THE TWO MAIN CURRENTS of feminism: reformist and radical, each had different yet significant influences on political parties, unions, and women's organizations.

While the small radical groups were engaged in feverish activity, the much larger membership of the Fédération des femmes du Québec was firmly convinced that lobbying rather than "revolutionary" action was the more effective strategy.

December 7, 1970 saw the publication of the Report of the Royal Commission on the Status of Women (the Bird Report). It was 540 pages long and contained 167 recommendations—abortion being one of its most controversial points. Seven sections concerned birth control and abortion, including Recommendation 126: "We recommend that the *Criminal Code* be amended to permit abortion by a qualified medical practitioner on the sole request of any woman who has been pregnant for 12 weeks or less."

However, the commissioners were not unanimous in their support of this recommendation. Two commissioners, Jacques Henripin and Doris Ogilvie, dissented. Meanwhile, another Commissioner, Elsie Gregory McGill, believed that the Commission had not gone far enough. She asserted, "In my view, abortion should no longer be considered an offence, but rather a private matter that concerns the physician and the patient."

The recommendations in the Bird Report had the potential to transform women's lives. They covered the economy, education, family, tax, poverty, political participation, immigration, nationality, and female offenders. Among them was the recommendation that no occupation should be closed to women. Soon, women would join the RCMP, police forces, and the armed forces.

The FFQ published a 46-page discussion guide to the Bird Report and distributed thousands of copies. Women led discussions across Québec. All the women's organizations, branches of AFÉAS (Association féminine d'éducation et d'action sociale) and Cercles de fermières, held countless meetings on the recommendations of the Bird Report. Although women were a long way from unanimity, the recommendations were gaining ground.

The Bird Report's final recommendation was to create an agency in every province that "would be concerned with the status of women and have sufficient authority and funds to make its work effective." The FFQ immediately set to work on this proposal. A committee drafted a rigorously documented brief entitled *L'Office de la femme* [the Women's Office] which they presented to Québec Premier and Liberal Party leader, Robert Bourassa, in November 1971. Adept strategists, some of the committee members were also members of the Fédération des femmes libérales. These women were veteran activists who were familiar with the methods for advancing their cause in the political arena; indeed, they had learned these methods within their own Liberal Party. Hundreds of copies of the brief were distributed amongst feminist and women's groups. The brief was also sent to all the government ministries and was translated into English.

The FFQ presented its brief to Premier Robert Bourassa in Québec City. The overview stated "Our brief is not presented in a spirit of confrontation, but rather out of concern that the agency proposed by the government will not have sufficient authority and that discrimination against women will be made worse." The FFQ worried that women would be viewed as a separate category of citizen. Claire Kirkland introduced the Bill creating the agency to the National Assembly and it was finally adopted on July 6, 1973. The new agency was named: the *Conseil du statut de la femme* (Status of Women Council). Its first president, Laurette Champigny-Robillard, was a member of the FFQ committee. Although the Liberal government created the Council, it was the members of the Fédération des femmes du Québec who had done all of the work.

Every year, the FFQ held a convention to set its priorities. Throughout the 1970s, these conventions served as occasions to share feminist information and to develop policy. Yet the word "feminist"

Simone Monet-Chartrand, a well-known activist, addresses one of the many conferences organized by the FFQ. From left to right: Ghislaine Patry-Buisson (president of the FFQ from 1974 to 1977), Monique Bégin (founding member), Yvette Rosseau (president from 1970 to 1974), Simone Monet-Chartrand (founding member) and Rita Racette-Cadieux (president from 1968 to 1970).

was rarely heard, because the term in Québec now referred to the radical feminists. The FFQ produced working papers, formed committees, organized information sessions, took part in conferences organized by other organizations, and, beginning in 1969, published a newsletter, the *Bulletin de liaison de la Fédération des femmes du Québec*. The FFQ concentrated its action on women's rights, education, family structure, paid employment, political involvement, social development, the environment, economics, and international issues. It was an ambitious program for change.

"The FFQ is a serious, reasonable, and determined organization," declared Yvette Rousseau, a member of the executive committee for eight years. Its members strove for a moderate tone and distanced themselves from the radical feminists. But the FFQ had to address the issue of abortion, an issue that divided the membership. What position would it take? The Conseil regional de Sherbrooke produced a brief which set out the legal, educational (sex education), economic, and social aspects of abortion and recommended that the FFQ support the right to abortion, framing it as a question of justice for women. The FFQ ratified this position at its next convention.

In 1974, preparations began for International Women's Year. On the urging of international feminist organizations, the UN had declared that 1975 would be the year for assessing the situation of women around the world. A journalist, Paule Sainte-Marie, was appointed to coordinate the activities women were organizing across Québec. Many activities were held: symposia, lectures, study days, and so on. That year, women were a hot topic in the media. The program *Femmes d'aujourd'hui* churned out interviews and news stories.

In 1975, FFQ president Ghislaine Patry-Buisson, went to Mexico City for the UN's first World Conference on Women, a huge international gathering of official delegations and non-governmental groups (NGOs). Over 10,000 women attended the meeting that had as its theme, "Equality, Development, and Peace."

Women from western countries represented the majority at this conference, leading one African delegate to declare, "You have to be rich to talk about feminism."

Despite their differences, women of the world united in powerful solidarity.

What have women in Québec accomplished since the early 1970s?

CHAPTER 22

Feminism Makes Waves

REGARDLESS OF WHETHER they were radical or reformist, all of the women's organizations had been influenced by feminist ideas since the early 1970s. Organizations flourished during this time because it was a time of generous government funding. All levels of government—federal, provincial, and municipal offered a broad range of programs that enabled women's groups to obtain funding for special projects. We should not underestimate the impact government funding had in the explosion of feminist initiatives. This funding was a boon for women's organizations such as the Centre des femmes, the Fédération des femmes du Québec, AFÉAS, and countless others.

POLITICAL ACTION

It was also during this time that women began to participate more actively in the major political parties in Québec. Droves of women joined the Parti Québécois as soon as it was formed in late 1968. A status of women committee strove to place women's concerns at the heart of the party's platform, but women were confronted with a fairly conservative current within the party. After a conference organized by the Montréal-Centre region, women realized that they would have to join forces. They created status of women committees in every riding and actively supported various feminist groups. These women became increasingly critical of their own party, especially when the Parti Québécois took power in 1976, raising the question whether it would be possible to combine feminism with mainstream political action?

In 1970, the members of the Fédération des femmes libérales were invited to join the Liberal Party in 1970; until then they had

refused any formal association with the Liberal Party. They negotiated the conditions of their joining to ensure that they were not pushed to the sidelines once they became members. Lise Bacon, President of the Fédération des femmes libérales, went to the party's General Council and proposed a formula to guarantee that women would have seats in the riding associations and on the main committees, particularly the strategically important Policy Committee that determined the party's platform, as well as seats on the Executive Committee. This way, women would have a say at all levels of the party structure, and, most importantly, it would ensure that women's objectives were included in the party's platform, although getting the desired results would not always be easy. As a result of this amalgamation, the Liberal Party doubled its membership.

Lise Bacon was elected to the National Assembly in 1973 as a Liberal. In 1985 she became the first female Deputy Premier, a position she held for eight years. Ms. Bacon was appointed to the Senate in 1994.

Despite the internal difficulties in promoting a feminist agenda, the Parti Québécois did contribute to the advancement of women's rights. When Louise Cuerrier became vice-president of the National Assembly in 1976, her title was feminized (*vice-présidente* instead of *vice-président*) consistent with an opinion issued by Québec's language office, the Office de la langue française. Inevitably, a burst of activity followed to feminize the language and job titles to reflect the fact that women were entering positions traditionally reserved to men. Québec quickly became a world leader in the feminization of the French language. Lise Payette was the first woman to be called "Madame la Ministre" when she became the Minister of State for the Status of Women in 1979. This process would not have occurred were it not for the pressure exerted by women activists within the Liberal Party.

Other women's groups brought their demands into the political arena. Aboriginal women had not forgotten the demands of Mary Two-Axe Early and her Mohawk sisters when they appeared before the Bird Commission. In 1974, the organization, Québec Native Women, was born, representing women of the First Nations in Québec and Aboriginal women living in urban areas. Their goal was the promotion of justice, non-violence, women's equal rights, and health. They also wanted to amend the antiquated *Indian Act*.

In Québec City the author, Marcelle Dolment, worked on women's legal issues. She was particularly outraged by the custom of identifying women by their matrimonial status: "madame" for married women and "mademoiselle" for single women. She recommended the abbreviation "Mad.," similar to the title of Ms. that American women were demanding. Although her proposal was not accepted, the custom was changed so that all women, even nuns, use the title "Madame." In 1973, Marcelle Dolment published *La femme au Québec*, and in the same year founded the *Réseau d'action et d'information pour les femmes* (RAIF) [Women's Action and Information Network], which published a magazine under the same name, featuring legal issues and media reviews. Branches of RAIF were created throughout Québec.

UNION ACTION

For the unions, the 1970s were a time of protest. Québec was experiencing major labour unrest in the early 1970s, with workers striking in the health and education sectors. Special legislation was passed in 1972 to defeat the Front commun [common front] of the three main labour federations (CSN, FTQ, and CEQ), and the three labour leaders were jailed. Women trade unionists pressured for the creation of women's committees in the three labour federations. These committees were now being called "comité-femmes" rather than "comité-féminin" (women's rather than feminine committee) and they began to play a central role in the feminist movement.

In 1973, the Fédération des travailleurs du Québec (FTQ) published a position paper titled "Travailleuses et syndiquées" [Women workers and unionists] which set out the demands of women workers. Beyond the traditional demands of maternity leave, daycare, and equal pay, the FTQ raised the issue of employment discrimination: why were women prevented from doing certain jobs?

The Women's Committee of the Confédération des syndicats nationaux (Confederation of National Unions or CSN), the new name for the CTCC, was formed in 1974. In 1976 CSN launched its policy platform: *La lutte des femmes, combat de tous les travailleurs* [women's struggle, the fight of all workers]. For female trade unionists, it was a major victory to have the entire membership endorse their demands. However, their writings were heavily influenced by the analysis of the Far Left; improving the status of women was tied to abolishing capitalism.

In 1973 women in the Centrale de l'enseignement du Québec [the Teachers' Federation], formed a Women's Committee, the *Comité Laure-Gaudreault*, named in honour of Laure Gaudreault, the founder of the female rural elementary school teachers' association. However, the Centrale did not publish its policy on women until 1980.

The labour federations took over the organization of International Women's Day events for March 8, 1974. But the Fédération des femmes du Québec and AFÉAS did not attend, because International Women's Day was still associated with the radical feminists.

SOCIAL ACTION

As the 1970s began, abortion was constantly in the headlines. This debate monopolized public attention for many years. The Assemblée des évêques [Assembly of Bishops], Cercles de fermières, some members of the Parti Québécois, and numerous pro-life groups stood firmly against abortion. In opposition, feminist groups in Québec and in many countries organized countless demonstrations,

The struggle for women's right to abortion was one of the biggest feminist campaigns of the 1970s. This demonstration, organized by the *Coordination nationale pour l'avortement libre et gratuit*, took place on April 22, 1978, in front of the National Assembly.

conferences, "study days," and protests. They pointed out that women were not against life, but rather for women's choice to have an abortion. Their slogan was: *Nous aurons les enfants que nous voulons.* [Our children will be wanted children.]

Demonstrations pitted pro-choice women against the pro-lifers. Dr. Henry Morgentaler was arrested and jailed several times and had to endure many trials, but he was always acquitted. January 1974 marked the beginnings of the Comité de lutte pour l'avortement libre et gratuit [Action Committee for Free and Accessible Abortion], with organizers from the recently closed Centre des femmes. It took the lead in this memorable and, as Louise Desmarais, one of its leaders, would say, "always unfinished" struggle.

Now, another group of women was demanding freedom and civil rights: lesbians. In the early 1970s, a strong wave of revolt against many forms of oppression was driven by the powerful social protest movements of the period. It was also the era of the "sexual revolution," which questioned traditional attitudes toward sexuality. Lesbians had been forced to live clandestine lives. If they did affirm their sexual identity, or if, despite careful precautions, they were identified as lesbians, they would often be rejected by their families, expelled from school, fired from their jobs, even arrested. Until 1969, homosexuality was a crime: not only a crime, but a sin, even a disease. By the mid 1970s, informal lesbian groups were created to provide lesbians with space to meet outside of the bars.

Lesbians were actively involved in many women's groups, including those seeking free and accessible abortion. Even though abortion was not an issue that affected many of them personally, lesbians understood it as another aspect of women's demand for control over their bodies and sexuality. They also sought economic independence for women. They refused to be economically dependent on men. In short, feminist demands corresponded to lesbians' desire to openly express their love for women.

Daycare was the main concern of the feminist social and political groups that proliferated during the 1970s. The struggle was no longer exclusively about working mothers' needs; it was also about their children's needs. The Québec government funded a few daycare centres in poor neighbourhoods. Daycares started appearing everywhere, funded by community groups, parents' groups, feminist groups, and unions. In the political arena, many continued to believe that daycare was not a government concern: "Women who want to work should just deal with it!" But, since the Bird Report had recommended the creation of a network of government funded daycare centres, it was inevitable that policy on the daycare issue would eventually have to be developed.

By late 1973, there were already over 250 daycare centres, most of them run by parents. The Local Initiatives Program funded 70 of these centres, but only ten of them received funding from Québec's social affairs ministry. In 1974, Lise Bacon, now a Liberal government minister, launched the first, very modest, governmental daycare program: financial assistance for parents and start-up grants for non-profit daycare centres. This was a far cry from feminist demands for a full network of daycare centres. But daycare was not a priority for the Liberal Party. At its convention in April 1976, the party threw out a proposal for the creation of a broad-based daycare network without discussing it, recommending instead a generous family allowance program. The battle for daycare was on.

Meanwhile, women at AFÉAS were in heated debate. Was AFÉAS a women's or a feminist association or was it a family-based

Azilda Marchand (1918-2010) was the co-founder of l'Association feminine de l'éducation de l'action sociale, serving as its president from 1970 to 1975. She focused AFÉAS on the invisibility of women's work and the need to recognize its worth.

group? Its members, the vast majority of them mothers, were disconcerted by the behaviour of their teenage children (the young "hippies" of the 60's and 70's). For the time being, they prudently decided to stay out of the abortion debate. While these discussions were going on, AFÉAS's president, Azilda Marchand, believed there was a much more important problem to consider: the invisible work of women. She was very disappointed in the Bird Report: "They [have] ignored rural women and women who work in their family's business."

Thanks to Azilda Marchand, in 1974, AFÉAS began documenting the invisible work of women who were soon to be known as the *femmes collaboratrices* [women partners] in the family business, especially farms. Published in 1976, AFÉAS's report transformed the lives of women in rural areas and gave rise to demands that would result in their being considered "real" workers.

Were these initiatives affecting the wider population of women?

CHAPTER 23

Domestic Violence and Assistance for Women

OF COURSE, not all women were interested in political or union activism. The majority of women were a little unsettled by what they heard about feminism from the newspapers, magazines, radio, and TV. Many women were so heavily burdened by their personal financial problems that they had little time to think about feminism.

These women nevertheless got together to talk about their problems and to try to resolve them. Since women had obtained the right to social assistance, single mothers (no longer called "unwed mothers") were no longer compelled to give up their babies for adoption and now faced the enormous challenge of raising their children on meagre social assistance cheques. Under the law, their children did not belong to them. Unmarried women had to adopt their own children in order to have them legally considered their legitimate children. Most women lacked the information required to go through this process but when they got together they could share information, organize, and work on these issues.

Since access to divorce had been expanded in 1969, the number of separated and divorced women had steadily increased. Most of them had custody of their children and were in dire financial straits. During this period, it was still extremely humiliating for a woman to be divorced or separated. In 1970, women in Montréal founded *Séparées anonymes* or ANO-SEP, a group based on the model of Alcoholics Anonymous. Separated women shared their experiences and offered each other a form of group therapy.

In 1973, a separated mother in Sherbrooke initiated a "teach-in," a day-long conference with speakers on single-parent families. Experts came to discuss the problems confronting these families. In the room, hundreds of women realized they could support each other and defend their rights. They created the *Carrefour des familles monoparentales*. In 1974, they were joined by the women of ANO-SEP. Soon, it had offshoots throughout Québec and by 1976, some 60 groups had formed in 39 cities. It was not long before these groups started exploring other feminist ideas.

In 1974, at Montréal's Institut Notre-Dame de la Protection, the women's shelter founded in 1932 by Yvonne Maisonneuve during the Depression, women realized that they would have to adjust to the new social context. They changed the name of their shelter to *Le Chaînon* [the link]. Most often, the women who came through their doors were fleeing a battering husband.

Elsewhere in Québec, similar solutions to domestic violence were evolving. In Longueuil (south of Montréal), a volunteer with the Service diocésain de l'aide aux familles welcomed to her office a woman and her children who had nowhere to go for the night after her husband had beaten her. There were no local services for women in such a situation. After finding a temporary solution for her, the volunteer lost touch with the woman. But she was determined to do something about the situation. She got together with other women and decided to open a women's shelter. By late 1975, *Carrefour pour elle* [A Place for Her] had opened its doors in Longueuil.

In Sherbrooke, members of the single mothers' group, the *Association des familles monoparentales*, discovered that many of them had lived with a violent husband. The leaders of the group decided they needed a house to shelter women fleeing from abuse. After much negotiation, surveys of social services, and grant applications, they obtained a house from the school board. However, the women seeking shelter weren't allowed to stay there overnight. At last, with the assistance of nuns in the order of Filles de la Charité du Sacré-Cœur, they managed to obtain a house where several mothers and their children could be properly sheltered. The house, called *Escale de l'Estrie*, opened its doors in 1975.

"These transition houses were created because there were no institutions responding to the needs of battered women," says Madeleine Lacombe, one of the first activists to take up the issue of male violence.

Of course, the phenomenon of battered women was not new. Women had spoken tentatively about the subject in feminist circles of the early 20th century. In the Fédération nationale Saint-Jean-Baptiste, women used the term *abus de force* [abuse of strength]. In that era, feminists had campaigned against alcoholism as a way of addressing the problem of domestic violence, characterizing the problem as a private matter. Rarely had women reported their husbands' abuse to the authorities. Most of them, totally financially dependant on their husbands, had simply endured it, because divorce was impossible. Not a single line of the Bird Report had been devoted to this issue.

In the 1970s, when women began separating from their husbands and daring to talk with each other about their experiences, everything changed. The taboo surrounding domestic violence finally began to lift. New homes for "battered women," as they were called then, appeared throughout Québec, testifying to the fact that the problem was widespread. In 1976, there were ten houses; by 1978 there were 23. The women who went to these shelters were guaranteed complete confidentiality.

Feminists had to act before social attitudes would change but feminists were active and attitudes did begin to change. Feminists even succeeded in convincing those in religious circles to open refuges for women. Several radical feminist organizations also founded women's shelters. As their analysis of violence against women became much more focussed, many men were threatened by it. Feminism was making waves in all spheres of public life.

How would feminism influence the cultural scene?

CHAPTER 24

Artists Explore Feminism

AS WE HAVE SEEN, the early 1970s were marked by an explosion of feminist activities. Many people believe, for good reason, that feminism was born during that period. When people talk about the feminist revolution of the 1970s, they usually mean the flurry of feminist cultural creations during that period. There were so many innovative cultural events during those years that it is impossible to describe them all. Feminism influenced women in every artistic domain: film, theatre, literature, song, and visual arts. In this exceptional climate, feminism touched women of all backgrounds, even those who paid no attention to the "status of women." Suddenly, women were no longer simply the muses and inspiration of male artists; they were the subjects of their own creative work.

CINEMA BY WOMEN FOR WOMEN

In 1972, women film directors began to emerge, and they were making films about women. For decades, women had worked in cinema, but they had been invisible, relegated to secondary roles behind the directors and subjected to the gaze of the men behind the cameras. In 1972, 13 women—directors, producers, screenwriters and assistants—formed a working group and during a six-month period, met with women of different ages. All the meetings were filmed and the conversations, some touching on very intimate topics, sparked a series of films produced by the National Film Board: *En tant que femmes* [As Women].

"Women from the suburbs came to our meetings saying they were perfectly happy. By the end, they were no longer so sure. Their happiness had come at the price of their individuality," remembers filmmaker Anne-Claire Poirier, one of the discussion leaders.

Women used all the film genres: documentaries, features, short films. By 1973, three films had been launched. When Aimée Danis' *Souris, tu m'inquiètes* [Smile, You Worry Me] opened in movie theatres, thousands of suburban women immediately identified with the film. When Mireille Dansereau's *J'me marie, j'me marie pas* [I'm getting married; I'm not getting married] appeared, her critical view of marriage challenged public opinion. *À qui appartient ce gage?* [A children's game] by a collective of five directors, thrust the issue of daycare beyond feminist activist circles into the public domain.

Anne-Claire Poirier was one of the most important filmmakers in Canadian history. Her best known film, *Mourir à tue-tête* (A Scream From Silence), was selected for the 1979 Cannes Film Festival. In 1996 she directed *Tu as crié: Let me go*, a documentary which dealt with the murder of her daughter and was awarded a Genie.

"We rarely heard women say 'Me' or 'I'," remembers Anne-Claire Poirier. "For us, that was the most distressing realization."

In her melancholy 1974 film on the history of women in Québec, *Les filles du Roy* [The King's Daughters] (*They Called us "Les filles du Roy,"* in the English version), Anne-Claire Poirier presents a succession of photographs of men while a woman's voice murmurs "My son the judge, my son the priest, my son the doctor, my son the minister." In another sequence, women are seen taking care of

In this era of exciting political theatre, there were lots of collectively written plays. In 1976, *La Nef des sorcières* [The Witches' Nave] was a major success. Cast members were also involved in the writing process. From left to right: Pol Pelletier, Michèle Magny, Françoise Berd, Louisette Dussault, Michèle Craig and Luce Guilbeault.

children while we hear, "I console, I take care of, I hug, I feed, I rock, I …" Women left this film devastated by the realization that their lives were not really their own.

In Hélène Girard's film, *Les filles, c'est pas pareil* [It's Not the Same for Girls], which also came out in 1974, teenage girls discuss love and friendship. They do not accept the submissive role that is expected of them. They do not want to be like their mothers. When the filmmakers encountered a group of women aged 65 and older, they were told: "So many of us got taken in. Good for them [the younger women], if they don't suffer what we had to suffer."

Finally, in 1975, Anne-Claire Poirier made *Le temps de l'avant* (*Before the Time Comes*), a wrenching feature film about abortion. This series of films had an enduring impact on women in Québec. Later, numerous other films took up the issues being raised by feminists. A few will be mentioned in later chapters of this book.

THEATRE AS A FORUM FOR SOCIAL CHANGE

Many women involved in women's groups during this time decided to use theatre to put feminism on the map. In 1975, former members of the Front de liberation des femmes and the Centre des femmes founded the *Théâtre des cuisines* [Kitchen Theatre]. They chose this name to evoke women's invisible and free labour. Their first play, a collective work, was all about housework with a title borrowed from humorist Yvon Deschamps: *Môman travaille pas, a trop d'ouvrage* [Mom has no job, she works too much]. This troupe existed for several years and presented numerous plays.

In 1976, many actresses who were involved with the Théâtre expérimental de Montréal put on plays about women. The last one, a collective creation called *À ma mère, à ma mère, à ma mère, à ma voisine* [To my mother, to my mother, to my mother, to the woman next door] was a turning point for many of them. They went on to found the Théâtre expérimental des femmes in 1979. For five years, this group, led by Pol Pelletier, made an indelible mark on the Montréal theatre scene.

During this time, three plays attracted particular attention. They were presented by the Théâtre du Nouveau Monde: *La Nef des sorcières, 1976* [The Witches' Nave], another collective work; *Les fées ont soif, 1978* [The Fairies are Thirsty] by Denise Boucher; and *La Saga des poules mouillées, 1981* [The Saga of the Wet Hens] by Jovette Marchessault.

Les fées ont soif presents a wife, a prostitute, and the Virgin Mary, three facets of "woman." They each cry out their anger at being forced into a pre-defined mould. The president of Montréal's arts council refused to fund the play, calling it "rubbish." The play premiered in Montréal on November 25, 1978 and was immediately denounced by religious authorities. Many Catholic groups protested during the performances, including the Cercles de fermières. A coalition of Catholic organizations obtained an injunction from the Superior Court of Québec prohibiting the publication of the play. The debate was so heated that sales of the play increased and countless copies were snatched up. Spurred on by the scandal and scores of articles, both positive and negative, published in all the media, the play became a huge success. In January 1979 the playright, Denise Boucher, and the Théâtre du Nouveau Monde were ultimately successful in persuading the Court to reverse its decision and overturn the injunction.

The theatre was an important forum of expression for feminists. From 1974 to 1980, and especially after 1977, some 25 women's productions, most of them collective creations, were seen by audiences across Québec. In the spring of 1980, the first *Festival de creations de femmes* was a hit, featuring 15 shows, four performances, two lectures, four films, two concerts, one video screening, and 12 workshops. Over 1,000 people from all walks of life took part. These theatrical productions provided opportunities for women to experiment with possibilities unavailable to them in the traditional theatre. And these new perspectives on women's lives encouraged many women to become feminist activists.

WOMEN WRITERS

As early as 1975, women writers convinced the organizers of the Rencontre québécoise internationale des écrivains to organize their annual conference on the theme of women and writing, "La femme et l'écriture." It was well attended by writers of both sexes from everywhere in the Francophonie [French-speaking countries].

"I'm sorry to have to say that, at the moment, literary organizations, and I'm not accusing anyone in particular, are in the hands of men," declared author Madeleine Ouellette-Michalska.

"It took me a few months to write my most recent book. It then took me four years to get it published," added journalist and author Monique Bosco.

This gathering was a turning point in Québec literary life. Women poets, novelists, and essayists began to experiment with the very act of writing, creating a style that embraced modernity, liberating itself from codes, grammar, literary forms, and prescribed models. "The act of writing 'I am a woman' has many repercussions," proclaimed poet and novelist Nicole Brossard, who became a leading voice of this new literary current.

Women wrote provocative pieces on the status of women, feminist activism, female-male relationships, lesbianism, intimacy, and the imagination. These authors affirmed that women are persons, rather than objects as seen through the male gaze. Women's writing became the central phenomenon of literature in Québec.

The audience of most of these works rarely extended beyond literary circles, but in 1976, *L'Euguélionne* became an instant best-seller. It was the first book to capitalize on the popularity of feminism in its marketing strategy. Author Louky Bersianik (pseudonym for Lucile Durand) had written a work that blended many literary genres: fable, theory, fiction, humour, polemic. She invented a

Lucile Durand refused to perpetuate the patriarchal custom of women taking their father's last name and named herself Louky Bersianik. In 1976, she published *L'Euguélionne*, the first Québec book to identify itself on its cover as feminist. It was an instant success.

mythical character, the Euguélionne, who landed on Earth and was amazed by the status of women on Earth. Women devoured this provocative book, while startled male readers hesitated to be overly critical. A woman from a working class neighbourhood asserted, "Reading *L'Euguélionne* changed my life."

Durand chose the pseudonym Louky Bersianik, because she opposed the patriarchal custom of forcing girls to take their father's name. She chose a name that rejected all the rules.

WOMEN AND SONG

And this was not all. Ever since Clémence DesRochers had summoned together female singers and actresses to produce the revue *Les Girls* in 1969, more and more female singer-songwriters and stand-up comics began to address feminist issues in their performances. In 1972, Jacqueline Barrette became famous with her monologue *La Moman* which portrayed the alienation of working class women. Clémence DesRochers introduced a series of women characters: *la fille de factrie* [factory girl], waitress and labourer, who raised public awareness of the situation of working class women. Pauline Julien performed songs of rage and tenderness. Diane Dufresne was a

Francine Larivée created a
monumental installation that was
exhibited in a downtown Montréal
shopping mall in 1976, *La Chambre
nuptiale*. The piece was a radical
portrayal of marriage as a trap for
women. The matrimonial bed was
depicted as a casket.

rocker with a feminist bent. *"J'ai douze ans, maman!"*[Mom, I'm 12!] expressing the confusion of adolescent girls on the verge of womanhood is just one example.

VISUAL ARTS AS A MEANS OF FEMINIST EXPRESSION

Feminism also made its mark on the visual arts. The descendants of the signatories of the *Refus global* were now expressing feminist concerns. Of all the decade's creations, Francine Larivée's *La Chambre nuptiale* [the wedding chamber] was the most remarkable. This large-scale project, which took two years to produce, received the largest project grant for International Women's Year. It also received grants from programs associated with the Olympic Games, held in Montréal in 1976. Hundreds of people worked on its creation. The installation involved painting, sculpture, sound, and interaction with the public. Larivée's idea was to take the public on a journey into the womb. Exhibited in 1976 at the Complexe Desjardins, a downtown shopping mall, *La Chambre nuptiale* was seen by thousands of people every day. No one could fail to be affected by this critical vision of marriage.

"Marriage appeared to be the only acceptable path for women, but we were never told that it could also be a trap. That is what I wanted to show," explained Francine Larivée. She invested so much of herself in this project that it was seven years before she could create another work.

In 1973, an art gallery began devoting itself exclusively to the work of feminist artists. The Powerhouse Gallery in Montréal was the first women's artist-run centre in Canada and it quickly became the hub of feminist art projects.

All of this work received regular coverage on radio and TV. Women directors, hosts, and researchers were inspired by the variety of these creations and they made sure to convey the feminist message everywhere. Viewers of this period will certainly remember Radio-Canada's Aline Desjardins from *Femmes d'aujourd'hui* and Lise Payette of *Place aux femmes* and *Appelez-moi Lise*. But underlying it all were the activists and artists who had been transforming society.

Many people thought, and some even hoped, that after International Women's Year, things would settle down.

What would happen to feminism after 1975?

CHAPTER 25

A Complex and Diversified Feminism

AFTER INTERNATIONAL Women's Year, there was a rush of new women's initiatives across Québec: "battered" women's shelters, rape crisis centres (known in Québec as *centres d'aides et de lutte contre les agressions à caractère sexuel* or CALACS), women's centres, and women's health collectives. Feminist magazines were started, "teach-ins" and conferences were organized, and new courses for and about women were offered in universities and colleges. At the same time, the Conseil du statut de la femme published its first studies.

In the mid 1970s, even wide circulation magazines got into the act. *Châtelaine* and its editor-in-chief Francine Montpetit openly endorsed the feminist movement. In October 1975, the magazine published an issue that was entirely devoted to feminist analysis under the theme *Je veux parler* [I want to speak], in total contradiction to the messages of its advertisers. It broke the record for newsstand sales. At *Le Maclean* (predecessor of *L'actualité*), Catherine Lord wrote a feminist column for several years.

People began asking "But what do women really want?" It had become more difficult to distinguish between radical and reformist feminism. Now most activists agreed on most issues: access to abortion, maternity leave, daycare, violence against women, pornography. In 1977, the theme of the Fédération des femmes du Québec convention was violence against women. The term *la femme* [the woman] was gradually being replaced by *les femmes* [the women] because, as feminists asserted, woman does not exist except in men's minds. In 1978, women set up a common front to demand a genuine maternity leave, as promised by the Parti Québécois when it was elected to form the government in 1976. Women were particularly concerned about the flaws in the 1978 maternity leave legislation, denouncing the fact that so many women workers had no access to it. In many workplaces, pregnancy still meant dismissal. The list of groups who supported the common front's manifesto was almost as long as the manifesto itself.

In 1975, a group of young feminists in Montréal founded the *Librairie des femmes* [Women's Bookstore] on Rachel Street, in the heart of the Plateau Mont-Royal neighbourhood. It quickly became the meeting place for the rising numbers of women who were passionately interested in women's issues. The bookstore hosted panel discussions and other events, and a café where women could meet and talk into the night. The Librairie des femmes was unquestionably the starting point of feminist activism for hundreds of young women. For almost three years, it was the nerve centre of feminism.

That same year, another women's collective decided to form a publishing house to publish writings by women activists and artists. With the problem of women's unpaid and invisible labour in mind, they decided to call themselves *les editions du remue-ménage*, written in lower-case to emphasize that the enterprise was collectively run. Their logo was a drawing representing women doing a multitude of domestic labour tasks. By 1976, they had published their first work, the play *Môman travaille pas, a trop d'ouvrage*. This was quickly followed by other plays. In 1978, they published the first *Agenda des femmes*, an excellent way to support the publication of analytical writings.

MORE FEMINIST INITIATIVES

Also in 1975, activists opened the *Centre de santé des femmes du Plateau Mont-Royal*, the first in a network of women's health centres that subsequently appeared across Québec. They believed that women should take control of their own health and they criticized women's treatment at the hands of conventional medicine and doctors. Studies were showing that the medical system was too quick to propose surgery for women. In fact, one of the slogans of the period was *Il n'y a pas d'utérus assez bon pour être conservé ...* [No uterus is worth saving ...] Other studies established that doctors were over-prescribing drugs to women.

These activists denounced the medicalization of pregnancy, childbirth, and menopause. They proposed vaginal self-exam for women, using a speculum and a mirror. The psychological impact on women participating in these groups was profound.

The first birthing centres were created. Women explored new issues of women's solidarity in the group *Naissance-Renaissance*, which was formed in 1977. Groups were established for midwives and the long fight to enable midwives to practise their profession began another long, drawn out battle, like the struggles for abortion and daycare.

Hundreds of women who had previously "chosen" to stay at home to raise their children now wanted to enter the labour market. Birth control had made it possible to have fewer children. Would women now have full access to the paid work force? Or would they want to go back to school to further their education? People began talking about *Nouveau depart* [New Start]. The Young Women's Christian Association (YWCA) launched the program in 1976. The aim was to equip a whole generation of women who had been prepared only for the role of wives and mothers, and now were either willing or forced to become financially and psychologically independent. In the CÉGEPs, the junior colleges, dozens of Nouveau départ programs were offered throughout Québec. There were even plans for women-only CÉGEP programs symbolically named *Repartir!* or *C'est à ton tour!* [Start over! It's your turn!]

By now it had become obvious that not all paid work was liberating. Many women did not even earn the minimum wage and were forced to work overtime. Community groups realized that most women workers were not unionized. Who would fight for the saleswomen, the waitresses, the domestic workers, the underpaid keypunch operators, and the garment workers? In 1976, activists founded *Au bas de l'échelle* (Rank and File) to defend the rights of non-unionized women workers. This group worked primarily on reforming sections of the *Labour Code* and informing women, many of them immigrants, of their rights.

Women in transition houses and CALACS realized that women were not socialized to physically defend themselves, so they began teaching women self-defence techniques, including wen-do classes. These classes became very popular, especially after a Radio-Canada program showed a group of women who, by the end of the class, were able to split a plank of wood in two, armed only with their fists and their determination.

LESBIANS

Lesbians, for their part, were particularly concerned about male violence and had become much more radical, affirming, "Feminism is the theory and lesbianism is the practice." They could not understand how women could live with men, marry them, have male lovers, or common-law partners. Lesbians did not mince their words with heterosexual women, addressing them as "you heteros."

Some young women identified themselves as "political lesbians." They claimed it was the only way to live in a patriarchal world that oppressed women. By the late 1970s, the participation of lesbians had increased dramatically, to the point that they were the majority of some women's groups. Some of these groups split as a result of their radical ideas about patriarchal violence. Although it was a minority voice, this theme had a major impact. As one heterosexual feminist recounted, "We were supposed to talk to each other, express our resentments, criticisms and feelings concerning every aspect of our lives ... talk about our problems, first as feminists and second as lesbians or heterosexuals." She added, "This is how we were supposed to find out what was preventing us from moving forward in a unified way. It was very tense."

It would be a long time before this tension between heterosexual and lesbian feminists would abate.

FOUNDING OF THE REGROUPEMENT DES FEMMES QUÉBÉCOISES

In 1976, the first anniversary of the founding of the Librairie des femmes, the hub of feminist action in Montréal, was celebrated with a momentous evening. It was attended by many activists from the Parti Québécois who had quit their ridings' status of women committees. The leader of the PQ, René Lévesque, had used his veto to affirm that he did not feel bound by the convention's decision to include the right to free and accessible abortion in the party platform. Nationalist feminists were furious. The energy generated by this celebration inspired Andrée Lavigne, Denise Lavigne and

Andrée Yanacopoulo to rally together all the feminist forces then dispersed among a broad range of small groups. The new association was called the *Regroupement des femmes québécoises* [Coalition of Québec Women].

"We want independence, but we want it to happen with us and for us. In other words, women have to stop licking stamps for the PQ before independence, if they don't want to find themselves back in the kitchen after independence," declared the founders.

At its founding convention in 1978, the Regroupement des femmes québécoises made violence against women a priority. Membership quickly grew. The Regroupement joined other feminist activists in organizing major demonstrations.

The Dalila Maschino incident galvanized feminists in April 1978. Dalila Maschino, an Algerian woman, was kidnapped by her family, who refused to recognize her marriage in Montréal, and forced her to return to Algeria. This event thrust the issue of immigrant women's rights into the public spotlight. Feminists united and took to the streets in support of Dalila Maschino.

Anne-Claire Poirier's film about rape, *Mourir à tue-tête* (*A Scream From Silence,* in the English version), sparked a major social debate. Every screening was a happening. The Regroupement des femmes québécoises organized a Women's Tribunal on rape in June 1979 that was attended by 750 women. The impact of this Women's Tribunal was considerable. The members of the jury were not "extremists." They included a therapist, a family doctor, a legal scholar, an Ursuline theologian, and a lawyer. Testimonies erupted spontaneously from the audience. It was very emotional, with tears and angry outbursts. After the Women's Tribunal, the issue of male violence against women was central to the feminist movement, which almost certainly played a role in fostering the impression that feminists hated men.

FEMINIST MAGAZINES

This overview of diverse initiatives would be incomplete without mentioning the explosion of the feminist press during this time. The *Bulletin de la FFQ* (the FFQ newsletter, known as *La Petite Presse* in 1980, and still being published today) was joined by a number of other magazines.

The Fédération des femmes du Québec published the *Bulletin de la* FFQ from 1969 to 1980. It took the name of *La Petite Presse* in 1981. But the Montréal daily newspaper *La Presse*, which had chosen this title for a youth-oriented magazine, prohibited the FFQ from using it at the end of the 1980s. The FFQ then found itself without a magazine for several years, much to the dismay of its supporters.

A radical feminist publication, *Les Têtes de pioche*, was published between 1976 and 1979. It covered all the new feminist debates: wife battering, sexist advertising, lesbianism, daycare, rape, women's health, etc. This issue on women's work, published in May 1977, contained pieces on radical feminist thinking about maternity and housework.

Communiqu'elles, launched in 1974, was published in French and English by the Centre des femmes de Montréal until 1991. *Les Têtes de pioche* [Hard-headed Women] was published ten times a year from March 1976 to June 1979. It was produced by a collective whose members had backgrounds in literary circles and community groups. They explained the title of their revue as follows: "'*Les*' for our solidarity. '*Têtes*' because in this matter, the heart is not enough. '*Pioche*' for our stubbornness." This journal was central to feminist activism and thought for three years. However, like the fate of *Québécoises deboutte*, five years earlier, it did not survive the challenges of diminishing funding and intense ideological divisions.

The first issue of *L'Autre Parole* [The Other Word] also appeared in 1976. This little magazine, still in existence today, was

Many feminist magazines were published after the demise of *Têtes de pioche*. *Pluri-elles* (1978-1979) became *Des luttes et des rires de femmes* (1979-1982). There was also *Communiqu'elles*, from the Centre des femmes de Montréal and *L'autre parole*, published by Christian feminists.

the mouthpiece of Christian feminists critical of the Church who were trying to feminize theology and the liturgy. They succeeded in reaching many women. Its readership included women theologians, nuns, and pastoral educators. Feminist thinking had now penetrated all sectors of society. The presence of these Christian feminists surprised many other feminists for whom the Church was viewed as a misogynist institution.

Pluri-elles, which first appeared in 1977, published radical feminist writings, especially on women's control of their own bodies. This grass roots publication was rapidly succeeded by *Des luttes et des rires de femmes* (women's struggles and laughter), a much more professional journal published by a collective that had managed to obtain funding. The review existed from 1977 to 1981, always providing well-documented pieces. Like many of the magazines that preceded it, *Des luttes* stopped publication as a result of political differences.

A COMPREHENSIVE POLICY OF THE QUÉBEC GOVERNMENT

The accomplishments of the *Conseil du statut de la femme* should not be overlooked. Founded in 1973, its first president, Laurette Champigny-Robillard, oversaw the creation of its three divisions: information, research, and public education. Most importantly, she was responsible for initiating several studies on behalf of an

interministerial committee that led to the publication of a key document in September 1978: *Pour les Québécoises, égalité et independence* [For Québec women, equality and independence]. Serving as the foundation for the government's women's equality policy, this paper was the product of contributions from 116 women's groups across Québec. For the first time, official data existed that supported various dimensions of Québec women's struggles for education, equal pay, and health services.

The next president of the Conseil to be appointed, in late 1978, was Claire Bonenfant. She oversaw the publication, starting in 1979, of *La Gazette des femmes*. Since the magazine was initially free, each issue had an impressive print run of 50,000.

Laurette Champigny-Robillard was the first president of the Conseil du statut de la femme (1973-1978). Under her leadership the Conseil created the FSC *Bulletin* about women's rights which was distributed throughout Québec, created the Service Action—Women to be a clearinghouse and to provide services to women and co-ordinated the activities in Québec to celebrate International Women's Year (1975). Ms. Champigny-Robillard served as the first president and CEO of the Office of Disabilities Québec from 1978 to 1986.

By the end of the 1970s, almost every woman in Québec had been affected in one way or another by feminism—either through reformist feminism, which sought to improve social conditions, or through radical feminism, the goal of which was to transform society. The women's movement, which was much less political, had provided a multitude of services for women on all fronts.

After the victory of a sovereigntist party in 1976, the Parti Québécois, women were concerned about another burning issue. Since 1969, many feminists, especially those who identified with the

In 1979, the Conseil du statut de la femme launched its magazine, *La Gazette des femmes*. The title was taken from one of the first magazines put out by women's rights activists in France in the 19th century. Initially distributed free of charge, the magazine has been sold at newstands and by subscription since 1994 and continues to enjoy a loyal readership.

radical movement, linked the two issues: women's liberation and the liberation of Québec. This had been the rallying cry of the Front de liberation des femmes in 1969.

Feminists were divided on the sovereignty issue. All feminist activists were politically astute and were aware of the importance of engaging in political debates. However, sovereignty was unacceptable to many reformist feminists. Since the mid 1960s, these feminists had proclaimed their political neutrality about nationalism.

Could feminists stay out of the nationalist debates generated by the 1980 referendum campaign?

CHAPTER 26

Divided by the 1980 Referendum

BY 1980, THE OVERRIDING TOPIC of discussion on the streets was the referendum on the sovereignty of Québec. In 1976, Québecers had elected the first sovereigntist party to form the government after over a decade of social, cultural and political ferment out of which emerged a renewed and vital pride in the Québécois identity and the French language. Now, Québecers were being asked to decide: should Québec remain a member of the Canadian Confederation, or should it become a country in its own right? Feminists asked whether they should abandon their tradition of political neutrality and take a position on the question of sovereignty? Before seeing how this question resolved, we will take a quick look at the position of women in the political sphere.

As we have seen, women had won the right to vote in Québec in 1940, but a woman was not elected to the National Assembly in Québec until 1961. This was Claire Kirkland, a member of the Liberal Party. She served as a minister in various departments until 1973. That year, a second Liberal woman, Lise Bacon, was elected.

In the 1976 election that brought the Parti Québécois into power, five women were elected. Lise Payette, Louise Cuerrier, Denise Leblanc and Jocelyne Ouellet were elected for the Parti Québécois. Thérèse Lavoie-Roux was elected for the Liberal Party. In 1979, Lavoie-Roux was joined by Solange Chaput-Rolland. After most women got the vote in federal elections, it was more than half a century before any woman from Québec was elected to the House of Commons. In 1972, three Québec women were elected for the Liberal Party: Albanie Morin, Monique Bégin, and Jeanne Sauvé.

Many of these women, in their own way, expressed feminist views. This was particularly true of Claire Kirkland, who led the

Lise Payette was elected for the Parti Québécois in 1976. She had a strong feminist reputation because of her television and radio programs. A media veteran, she was a determined voice for women's demands with her less than enthusiastic Cabinet colleagues.

work on Bill 16 in 1964 (which enshrined the principle of equality between the spouses) and the Conseil du statut de la femme in 1970; Lise Bacon, who negotiated the conditions for integrating the Fédération des femmes libérales into the Liberal Party and supported the first governmental daycare program; Monique Bégin, one of the founders of the Fédération des Femmes du Québec, who then served as secretary of the Bird Commission; Jeanne Sauvé, who fought for women's employment rights; Solange Chaput-Rolland, who was an activist in Voix des femmes [Voice of Women], and Lise Payette, who supported feminist issues, particularly abortion, on her TV show *Place aux femmes*, and who, in 1980, became the Minister Responsible for the Status of Women in the Québec government.

The Fédération des femmes du Québec (FFQ) and the Association féminine d'éducation et d'action sociale (AFÉAS) had, since their inception, adhered to the principle of political neutrality, while most independent women's groups were overtly sovereigntist in their political affiliations. In 1980, two activists attempted to form a committee at the FFQ to study the question of the referendum, but President Sheila Finestone rejected their proposal on the grounds of the Fédération's non-partisan tradition. It was a secret to no one, however, that many members of the Fédération were Liberal sympathizers. Meanwhile, AFÉAS stuck to their position of strict political neutrality.

Remember, the first slogan of the Front de libération des femmes du Québec was: *Pas de libération des femmes sans libération du Québec. Pas de libération du Québec sans libération des femmes.* [No women's liberation without the liberation of Québec. No liberation of Québec without women's liberation.] The Regroupement des femmes québécoises, founded in 1978, was frankly sovereigntist.

So, there was a feminist presence in both of the camps that were constituted in the spring of 1980: the OUI camp, comprising those who wanted Québec to separate and the NON camp for those who advocated staying in Canada. At the onset of the referendum campaign in January 1980, there was much enthusiasm for the sovereigntist camp and they won the debate in the National Assembly. Lise Payette concluded her address by declaring: "Speaking for myself, after giving children to this country, I'm working as hard as I can to give a country to these children!"

On the other side, those in the NON camp were very worried. Their leaders searched desperately for a winning strategy.

THE "YVETTES" AFFAIR

On March 8, 1980, International Women's Day, Lise Payette made a speech in the National Assembly in which she decried the sexist stereotypes still found in school textbooks: "Guy likes sports and dreams of winning lots of trophies. Yvette slices the bread, helps serve the roast chicken, and sweeps the rug. Yvette is a well behaved little girl."

She was determined to rid Québec women of those stereotypes that locked women into a passive role. The next day, at a meeting of party sympathizers, she again denounced the stereotypes in school textbooks that encouraged women to remain submissive and compliant homemakers: "We must have the courage to exit the prison of our fears." She added that the leader of the NON camp, Claude Ryan, head of the Liberal Party of Québec, wanted women to continue being Yvettes. "In fact," she said, "he's married to an Yvette."

The editor of *Le Devoir*, Lise Bissonnette, responded two days later, upbraiding Lise Payette for attacking a political leader through his wife: "Linking a woman to the personality of her husband, which hasn't been done since feminism's earliest days, is the height of

An "Yvettes" rally in
Sherbrooke. At the instigation
of women organizers with the
Liberal Party, women publicly
identified as "Yvettes" during
the first referendum campaign
on Québec sovereignty. This
was their response to Lise
Payette's statement associating
women in the NON camp with
the little girl, Yvette, a famous
school textbook character.

sexism." She further insisted: "In insulting Madeleine
Ryan, she is not only insulting Claude Ryan, but also
all those women whose equal rights she is supposed to
be defending."

Women working for the NON camp were insulted
by Lise Payette's remarks, which they understood to
mean they were incapable of independent thought.
Minister Lise Payette later apologized publicly for her
mistake: "If my remark hurt anyone, including the
wife of the Leader of the Opposition, I apologize, because this was
not my intention. My intention was to continue doing what I've
been doing for the past 20 years to help women in Québec destroy
these persistent stereotypes."

At this point, Liberal women realized they could turn this
controversy to their advantage by organizing a "Brunch des Yvettes."
They did it against the advice of party strategists, who considered it
dangerous to capitalize on a political error. One political strategist

commented, "It could have a boomerang effect, if it means that no one talks of anything else; it's like saying that we have nothing else to say."

Within 24 hours, Liberal women activists had rallied over 2,000 women to the "Brunch des Yvettes" in Québec City, where they heard speeches from Thérèse Casgrain, the famous feminist, and Thérèse Lavoie-Roux and Solange Chaput-Rolland, both Liberal members of the National Assembly, federal Health Minister Monique Bégin, and the wife of the Leader of the Opposition, Madeleine Ryan. All of them explained to the crowd why they were voting "no" and why they wanted to stay in Canada. Madeleine Ryan declared that she wanted to bequeath to her children a Canada with all of its parts. She added, "The *péquistes* [members of the Parti Québécois] want to use women, saying that women will be better off in an independent Québec when, in fact, there is no connection between the two issues."

This statement was practically the only reference they made to the situation of women. All of the speakers in the NON camp were silent on the subject of women, while in the OUI camp, women's independence was frequently linked to Québec's independence.

After their successful brunch, Liberal women activists followed up with numerous Yvette rallies. In Montréal, over 15,000 Yvettes gathered at a hockey arena, the Forum. Organizing this rally was a huge challenge: they had to obtain the party's authorization, prepare the site for the rally, sell tickets, charter buses, confirm speakers, print buttons, and collect masses of red carnations. Women in the Liberal Party handled it all. In the NON committee, FFQ President Sheila Finestone was responsible for getting authorization to hold the rally. Suddenly, the political neutrality of the FFQ had evaporated.

Large numbers of women enthusiastically attended all these rallies, proudly proclaiming that they were Yvettes. Louise Robic, the principal organizer, wanted no mention of Lise Payette and her comments in the speeches. The goal was to allow women who advocated the NON position to express their political position. All the speakers were feminists, from Thérèse Casgrain to Monique Bégin. In their speeches, they made absolutely no mention of feminist issues. When former FFQ president Yvette Rousseau took the microphone, she received an ovation—simply because of her name.

What was the driving force behind the "Yvettes"?

"They wanted to make fun of us. We'll show them that we can organize."

"We had to defend Madeleine Ryan, because she had been attacked."

"We wanted to show that we are capable. We women are pretty powerful."

"It was a way to get involved."

"It gave us the courage to say we were for the NON side."

"For me, it was an insult to my intelligence and sense of judgement. I didn't agree with the PQ, so automatically I was stupid."

A week later, more than 20,000 women and men gathered in Montréal for a sovereigntist rally to mark the 40th anniversary of women obtaining the vote. The speeches emphasized the importance of women having the right to vote, and related Québec independence to women's independence: a sovereign Québec would need its feminists.

CONCERNING THE REFERENDUM

Women activists at the Regroupement des femmes québécoises were divided. They were deeply disappointed by the Parti Québécois' attitude to feminist demands. After many tough discussions, they launched a campaign. The idea was to persuade women not to vote OUI or NON, but to write the word FEMMES on the ballot. This suggestion garnered little enthusiasm and in the end only a few followed their suggestion. The Regroupement des femmes québécoises never recovered from this failure.

These events received much media attention. Many journalists affirmed that the Yvettes were above all homemakers who were protesting against the supposedly exaggerated feminism of Lise Payette and a few "doctrinaire" feminists. Others tried to pit feminists against "real women," that is women who worked for a living against women who stayed at home. The following summer, a Radio-Canada report made much of this so-called division between stay-at-home women and feminists. Yet, many later studies have shown that the "Yvettes" phenomenon was above all linked to the referendum debate, enabling women who had never been politically active to express their views publicly. Indeed, they were so effective, they contributed to the victory of the NON camp on May 18, 1980. Nearly 58 per cent of women and men in Québec voted "no" on the referendum. In the end, the women's vote was simply a reflection of the majority opinion.

Sovereigntists were very frustrated, and women sovereigntists even more so. For them, the Yvettes movement was totally incomprehensible. Paradoxically, federalists never publicly acknowledged the key role played by the Yvettes campaign in ensuring their victory. The Yvettes episode was difficult for both sides. Yet, it was really very simple: women had taken the initiative and jumped into the political fray. The traditional elites and analysts invested a lot of time trying to understand what happened and still believe that the Yvettes represented the rejection of feminism. And yet …

Feminists had never been so numerous and so active. But now feminists in Québec were less unanimous in their views, and their analysis diverged in relation to their objectives.

Would feminism suffer from the divisions created by the referendum?

1969   Creation of the Front de libération des femmes du Québec

1971   Report of the Royal Commission on the Status of Women
[Bird Report]

1971   Publication of *Québécoises deboutte!*

1972   Creation of the Centre des femmes

1972   Beginning of the National Film Board's series
En tant que femmes

1973   Creation of the Conseil du statut de la femme

1974   Creation of the Comité de lutte pour la contraception
et l'avortement libre et gratuit

1975   International Women's Year

1976   Publication of *L'Euguélionne* by Louky Bersianik

1976   Exhibition of *La Chambre nuptiale* by Francine Larivée

1976   Publication by AFÉAS of the Rapport sur les femmes
collaboratrices

1976   Publication of *Têtes de pioche*

1977   Publication of *Des luttes et des rires de femmes*

1978   Publication of the governmental women's equality policy,
Pour les Québécoises, égalité et indépendance

1978   Creation of the Regroupement des femmes québécoises

1978   Performance of the play *Les fées ont soif* by Denise Boucher
at the Théâtre du Nouveau Monde in Montréal

1978   Anne-Claire Poirier's film *Mourir à tue-tête* debuts,
followed by the Women's Tribunal on rape

1979   Launch of *La Gazette des femmes*

1980   Referendum on the sovereignty of Québec

5 | WORKING TO CHANGE THE WORLD 1981 TO 2012

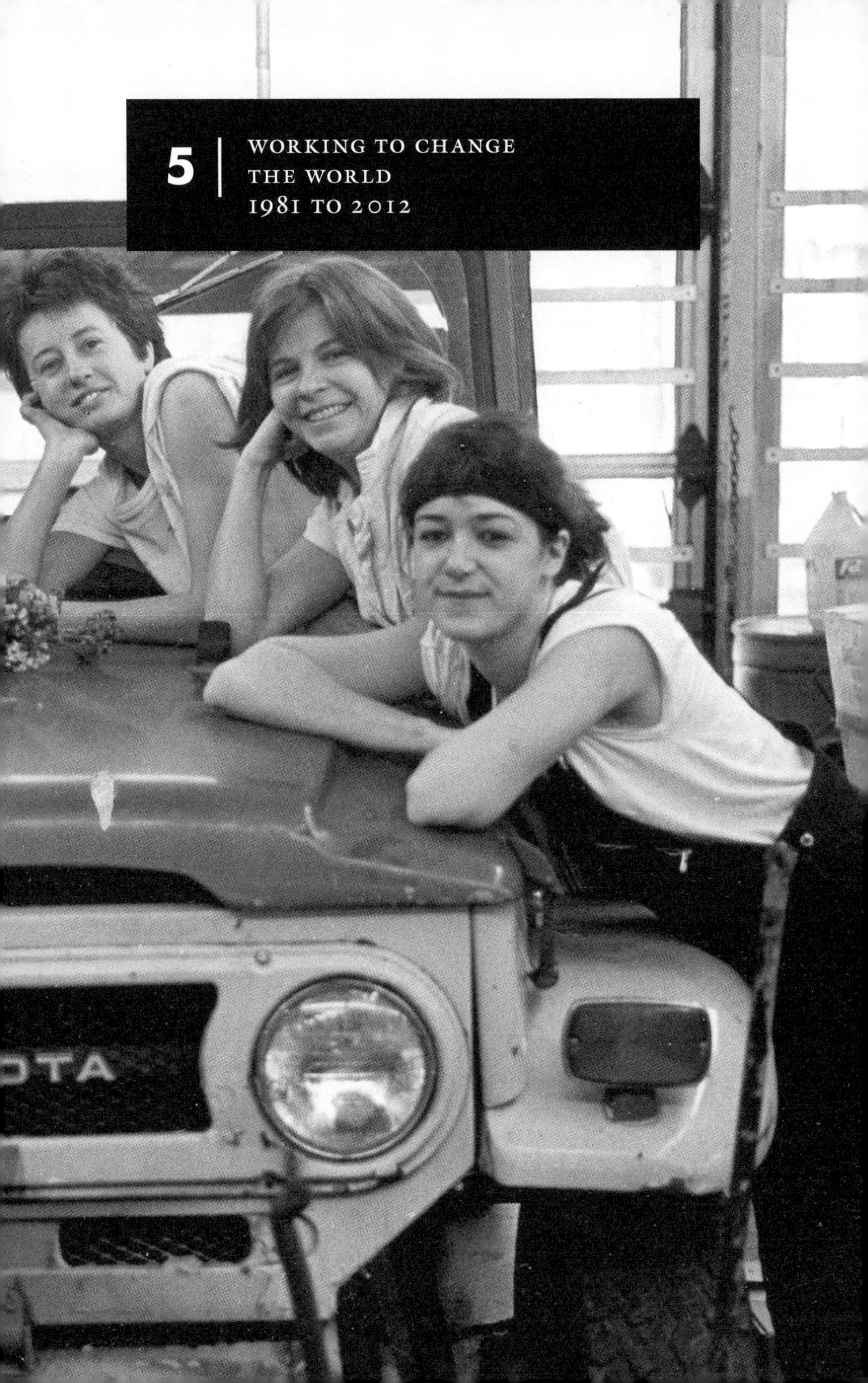

CHAPTER 27

The Transformation of Feminism

Feminist humourists, *Les Folles Alliées*, from Québec City include (from left to right): Lucie Godbout, Hélène Bernier, Christine Boillat, Agnès Maltais, Jocelyne Corbeil and Pascale Gagnon.

ON NOVEMBER 2, 1981, at the age of 85, Thérèse Casgrain told her loved ones she was going to bed early because she was leaving to attend a demonstration in support of First Nations women that was being held in Baie-Comeau the next day. Sadly, she never woke up. This tireless activist had worked for women's rights for over six decades.

Thérèse Casgrain's death signified the end of an era, the death of the last member of the group of feminists who had entered Québec public life at the turn of the 20th century. Her comment after the women's suffrage victory in 1940, "Our real work has just begun," was prophetic. Feminists did get to work—on an individual basis during the first generation, and collectively after 1966.

In 1925, Alexandre Taschereau, the Québec premier had declared, "If we give women the vote, we'll have to give mothers a pension." Feminists proved him right. Since they had won the vote and began identifying the multiple problems confronting women, they were now in a position to make demands of the government. It was all very well to change a few laws, but much work remained in order to change public attitudes. One example: The first time the issue of violence against women was raised in the House of Commons, on May 12, 1982, male politicians burst out laughing. And when feminists demanded an apology, they refused.

In the next 15 years after 1966, the feminist movement underwent a profound transformation. The 1970s changed everything, radical feminists transformed the list of women's demands. After calling for women's equal rights, feminists were now condemning the abuses of patriarchal society. New objectives quickly attracted feminists' notice. Women spoke out, demanding the right to control their bodies and denouncing all forms of violence against women. Activists discovered the hidden face of discrimination in the workplace. They became more concerned about poverty and the status of women of all social classes and origins. In Québec City, the *Secrétariat à la condition féminine* [Status of Women Secretariat] had been busy responding to women's needs since 1979. In Ottawa, Status of Women Canada was doing likewise.

The next four chapters describe the main aspects of feminist transformation in the 1980s.

VOLUNTEERS AND PAID WORKERS

For over 60 years, the feminist movement had depended on the volunteer commitment of women, primarily women with some financial means. Now, with the panoply of grant programs that feminists had managed to access and which would develop further throughout the 1980s, a broad range of services for women was gradually set up. Now women in all sectors of society would feel the influence of the feminist wave.

The feminist upheaval of the 1970s was followed by a period of significant feminist activity on various fronts. While many women were now able to find paid work in women's services, this did not mean that volunteers had left the women's movement. Far from it. Where would the Fédération des femmes du Québec be without the individual members who attended its yearly convention by the hundreds, prepared and studied policy papers, and mobilized in the regional councils? Where would AFÉAS be without its 30,000 members who met every month in their respective circles to discuss women's issues?

At the same time, a new form of feminist "expertise" was being developed—on the ground, in women's groups, at the administrative level, in government services, and in the universities where feminists were developing theory. Above all, changes occurred at the political level—in feminist associations, unions, and the mainstream political parties. Feminists were not unanimous in their analysis, but they were all well aware they had a huge job before them.

During the feminist upheaval of the 1970s, activists had wanted to get rid of structures. After 1980, this was no longer possible. Now,

Claire Bonenfant (1925-1996) was the president of the Conseil du statut de la femme du Québec from 1978 to 1984. The Conseil published *La Gazette des femmes*, a magazine providing information and news to women in Québec. In 1976 she produced the documentary *De femmes en filles*. In 1970, she had been arrested during the October Crisis.

every women's group had to have a charter, a board of directors, a coordinator, and minutes. Feminists integrated into civil society as providers of a variety of services. Many women who had never even learned "Feminism 101" got jobs in the women's movement.

But the grants only covered salaries for a few, and these salaries were usually ridiculously low. In every service group, scores of volunteers were needed to carry out day-to-day tasks, including running the women's shelters and women's centres, staffing the 24-hour rape crisis lines, and fundraising activities. And they were working for change—by holding policy sessions and writing briefs, reports, and articles of all kinds.

FEMINIST RESEARCH AND STUDIES

In 1979, the new president of the Conseil du statut de la femme (CSF), Claire Bonenfant, set up regional branches with the mission of coordinating the actions of women's groups, listening to the needs of women at the grass-roots level, and publishing the main findings of feminist research. These branches brought feminism to every region of Québec. The CSF played an essential role at that time in promoting feminist thinking. The CSF's magazine, *La Gazette des femmes*, was distributed free of charge, reaching a wide public. The studies commissioned and published by the CSF were read eagerly by feminist activists.

The CSF was not the only organization to produce research on the status of women. In the mid 1970s, universities and colleges set up women's studies courses that encompassed the disciplines of literature, sociology, theology, history, social work, anthropology, and political science.

In the feminist ferment of the 1970s, these courses were extremely popular. Instructors realized that these initiatives, usually individual, needed to be consolidated to prevent their eventual disappearance. Academics in the U.S. had set up women's studies programs. In Québec, professors created similar feminist teaching and research centres. Among them was the *Groupe interdisciplinaire d'enseignement et de recherche féministes* at the Université du Québec à Montréal (GIERF, 1976), *Institut Simone-de-Beauvoir* at Concordia University (1978), and *Groupe de recherche multidisciplinaire féministe* at Université Laval (GREMF, 1983). In no time, these centres were publishing research, publicizing new courses, starting up new journals, and organizing conferences.

Books, articles, and reports began appearing regularly. The feminist publishing house Les éditions du remue-ménage had a lot on its plate. It is difficult to determine the impact of this research because much of the work was never seen outside feminist circles. The following exchange that took place in 1981 is a classic example of the ghettoization of feminist scholarship.

"Did you get the special issue of women and sociology?" a woman professor asked a male colleague.

"Yes, I gave it to my wife," he answered, as if it had nothing to do with him.

In addition, women's groups and university researchers were developing ties with each other. In 1982, an agreement was signed in Montréal between Relais-femmes and Université du Québec à

Montréal (UQAM), which enabled women's groups to engage the university in conducting research they needed for their activist work.

QUÉBEC-WIDE ORGANIZATIONS

During this time, women's groups had become extremely numerous, creating the need for mechanisms to share experiences, coordinate actions, and organize meetings.

The list of Québec-wide associations is truly impressive. For example, the rape crisis centres' association, the *Regroupement des centres d'aide et de lutte contre les agressions à caractère sexuel* (CALACS) numbered 40 groups. Some 100 transition houses for battered women organized themselves into two Québec-wide associations: the *Regroupement provincial des maisons d'hébergement et de transition pour femmes victimes de violence conjugale* (1979) and the *Fédération des ressources d'hébergement pour femmes violentées et en difficulté* (1986). The two associations collaborated freely to compare working experiences and to organize joint actions that educated the police, healthcare services, and social services on women's issues.

Québec's women's health centres established an association in 1985 called the *Réseau québécois d'action pour la santé des femmes*. Its influence on medical practices began to be felt. There was an immense amount of work to do on this front. Why were women the only ones responsible for their family's health? Why were women being prescribed so many drugs? Why were so many women suffering from depression? A ground-breaking essay on women's health published by the Conseil du Statut de la Femme, the *Essai sur la santé des femmes*, became the bible of the women's health groups.

And, of course, the women's centres, located in women's apartments or homes where women went for information, educational activities, counselling and training, founded their own association in 1985, naming it *l'R des centres de femmes du Québec*: "R" for Regroupement; "R" for Réseau; "R" for ère as in the era of the women's centres; "R" for aire as in space for women to take; "R" for air as in *Donnez-moi de l'oxygène!* [Give me oxygen] from the song of singer Diane Dufresne. Quite the program for these 85 centres!

Meanwhile, in 1984 women who were working in various

settings to facilitate women's access to the labour market decided to organize an association called the *Conseil d'intervention pour l'accès des femmes au travail* (CIAFT).

In 1986, shortly after the creation of these Québec-wide groups, the CSF released a study that counted a total of 473 women's groups in Québec. And even this list was incomplete. Feminists were very busy indeed. Thanks to these associations, feminists now had mechanisms that made it easier to conduct coordinated actions, even when they were not in agreement about their analysis. They protested regularly against government decisions and organized collective actions to speak in a unified voice.

In 1986, the FFQ and AFÉAS founded the *Groupe des 13*, composed of the 13 principal women's associations. The goal was to have a coordinating structure so that feminists as a group could respond to governmental policy or organize quickly to respond to current events. Given the number of groups and associations, people began to speak of them as "institutional feminism." Women's coalitions were gradually being formed in every region of Québec and feminism's influence was spreading. One of the indicators that activists were working together was that International Women's Day or *8 mars* was now celebrated across all of Québec.

With so much activity underway, which issues would feminists prioritize?

CHAPTER 28

New Feminist Goals

AFTER THE FERMENT of the 1970s, the feminist movement discovered additional goals and new partners appeared on the feminist scene.

BROAD-BASED FEMINIST ORGANIZATIONS

Broad-based feminist organizations became more necessary than ever before. Issues reappeared on the agenda, most of them emerging from radical feminist thinking: abortion, women's health, violence against women, pornography, and women's work.

Structural changes were needed to deal with the changes in the late 20th century. Women's groups no longer resembled those of the 1960s. The Fédération des femmes du Québec (FFQ) was still hard at work, with paid staff in place since 1974. The organization needed to improve its formal ties with new member groups. Slowly but surely, more groups joined the Fédération; from 1985 to 1989, the FFQ tripled its group membership, growing from 40 to 111 member groups.

Those who thought that FFQ members were more moderate than the 1970s radical feminists had to think again. The FFQ was involved in all the coalitions. At the end of her term as president of the CSF, Claire Bonenfant said, "When I mentioned that the Fédération des femmes du Québec thought this or that, the government trembled."

But media interest in feminism was waning. In April 1986, *Le Devoir* published a front-page article about REAL Women in Hull. (REAL stands for Realistic, Equal, Active, for Life.) REAL Women were the opposite of feminists. They opposed abortion, daycare, and the legalization of homosexuality, and they advocated women's return to the home. The movement was quite strong in the U.S., but in Québec it was virtually non-existent. Yet, the media coverage of this small group eclipsed that of a major conference organized by the teachers' union called *Des outils pour agir ensemble* [Tools for Collective Action]. Feminists were furious.

Ten days later, the FFQ marked its 20th anniversary with a major symposium and *Le Devoir* repeated itself, prioritizing an international pro-life conference being held in Montréal over the feminist event. "It was a real shock to women. The Fédération now had to watch out for this new radical right-wing ideology," said FFQ president Ginette Busque.

The editor of *Le Devoir* defended his position: "It's a new trend, outside the usual discourse; it's a movement that is growing considerably in Canada and becoming more visible."

The media seemed to be tired of stories about feminist struggles. This is why commemorating the 50th anniversary of women obtaining the vote was so important in 1990. Preparations for this event had begun in 1986, four years earlier.

At AFÉAS, women continued to focus on the needs of women in the home, who formed the majority of their membership. AFÉAS conducted a broad survey on the status of housewives that generated new information about their financial insecurity, power-sharing in families, their work and health. One homemaker admitted, "I find it really frustrating to always have to ask for money, even for a small purchase. It's even worse if you had been employed before getting married."

Why did people not consider housework as real work? AFÉAS drafted recommendations to recognize the work of women in the home by more than the sanctimonious expression "queen of the household": sharing of family income, protection of the family home, sharing of pension plans and adjustments to benefits in the case of divorce. There was even a demand to provide homemakers with the same benefits as those for paid workers. Those who had believed, at the time of the "Yvettes" episode, that homemakers were making a comeback and that feminism was on the wane, became confused. Now the homemakers were hitting the barricades. When the government passed the *Act Respecting Economic Equality of the Spouses* in 1989, few people remembered that this law was an

Vous êtes tous invités
à une soirée de solidarité
organisée par les centrales
syndicales CEQ-FTQ-CSN pour souligner
la journée internationale des femmes.

"SOLIDARITÉ ET ACTION"

8 MARS

HEURE: 19:30
ENDROIT: CENTRE PAUL SAUVÉ (salle de curling)

answer, 50 years later, to Marie Gérin-Lajoie's demand to the Dorion Commission in 1929: "Measures must be taken to ensure that the marriage contract contains at least a few benefits for the wife."

From here on, the AFÉAS leaders were much less reluctant to identify as feminists. But some of their members left this organization to join the *Association des femmes collaboratrices*, which AFÉAS had helped found in the late 1970s. Also, the membership of AFÉAS was aging. The next generation was late coming to the movement because by this time almost all young women had paid employment and, if they were mothers, were dealing with double duties at home and at work, with less time to devote to feminist activism.

UNION ACTION

Women trade unionists also realized they would have to join forces. Naturally, each labour federation conducted many actions of its own: conventions, symposia, study days, writing reports, drafting demands, etc. After several collective efforts to organize International Women's Day activities, a coalition of women trade union representatives, the *Intersyndicale des femmes*, was formed in 1977, with the support of the major labour federations. The Intersyndicale examined the main issues related to women's work: maternity leave, sharing housework, sexual harassment at work, women's access to non-traditional trades, systemic discrimination. A new issue was raised: Why were traditionally female jobs almost always less well paid than traditionally male jobs?

Le 8 mars [International Women's Day] was marked for the first time in Montréal by feminists with the Front de Libération des Femmes in 1971. For many years thereafter, the event was organized by a coalition of women's committees from the main labour centrals. This is the poster for 1982.

"Man needed to be a gardener. Requirement: driver's licence. Pay: $16 per hour."

"Secretary needed. Requirements: college diploma in office technology, fluency in English and French; mastery of word processing software. Pay: $12 per hour."

This pay gap was totally unfair. Feminists proposed a new concept: pay equity, the valuing of women's work in comparison with men's work. Another long battle on the horizon.

In 1988 Lorraine Pagé became president of the CEQ, the labour federation that brought together the teachers' unions. For the first time, there was a female labour leader; and she did not hesitate to express her feminist convictions.

NEW GROUPS EMERGE IN RESPONSE TO THE NEEDS OF SPECIFIC GROUPS OF WOMEN

On November 11, 1983 in Montréal, right after the Remembrance Day ceremonies honouring soldiers who died in war, a mysterious woman in black moved forward to place a wreath with the inscription: "For every woman raped in wartime."

Dana Zwonok, accompanied by a group of 40 women, men and children, repeated her action the following year, in remembrance of "all women victims of war." It was a pacifist and solemnly respectful gesture. A veteran's wife attending the official ceremony expressed interest in joining the new group, *Consœurs du souvenir* (Sisters in remembrance). Her husband threatened her, saying, "If you do that, I'll shoot you!"

This peace initiative was significant in many ways. First, it recalled the link that had always existed between feminism and pacifism. Secondly, it was a unifying cause that affected women all over the world. And lastly, it was a signal that immigrant women were taking part in the feminist movement in Québec. Only a woman from a war-torn country could have thought of this striking initiative that grabbed the media's attention.

The numbers of immigrant women in Québec were steadily increasing. They formed the majority of workers in the textile manufacturing industry. They also worked as domestic workers and cleaners. Many of them could not speak French. Some were highly educated, but unable to get a job in their field in their new country. They came from very different cultures, yet were confronted by many of the same problems as other Québec women. But they tended to be reluctant to join feminist groups in Québec, mainly because Québec feminists had the reputation of being radical and not valuing the family, which was so important to many of them. With differing experiences of the many forms that male dominance might take, immigrant women needed to gather amongst themselves to explore together the possibilities offered by feminism. In 1985, they opened the *Centre des femmes immigrantes* in Montréal. Groups in other cities with large immigrant populations came together to set up similar centres.

In 1980, lesbians, who had played such an important role in independent women's groups and feminist magazines during the 1970s, began to organize among themselves. They felt excluded from the new Québec-wide feminist organizations and decided to organize on the basis of their lesbian identity. On March 8, 1983, for the first time, there was a lesbian contingent in the International Women's Day march. They marched with coloured shields symbolizing, when they lowered their shields, their visibility. Two magazines were launched in 1982, *Amazones d'hier et lesbiennes d'aujourd'hui* [Amazons of Yesterday and Lesbians of Today], published until 1990, and *Ça s'attrape!* [It's Contagious!] which became *Treize* in 1984 and continued to be published until 2008. Lesbians also developed networks and community spaces. They asserted themselves as a social group with its own history, identity, and culture.

At the same time, First Nations women continued their organizing efforts, begun in 1974. They set up health centres and transition houses, with services specifically addressed to their needs. In 1985, after a long drawn-out process, the federal government passed *Bill C-31* (*An Act to Amend the Indian Act*), which allowed Aboriginal women to keep their Indian status if they married a non-Aboriginal man. But the law was controversial, even within the First Nations communities. "This law divides families," deplored one Aboriginal woman.

Unquestionably, the Catholic Church figured at the top of the list of misogynous institutions. Women were much more numerous than men in Church communities. They were indispensable to the Church, serving in almost all of the subordinate positions that kept the Church functioning. Now nuns had new responsibilities, including that of "parish priest," but of course without the right to celebrate the sacraments.

Many Christian feminists felt the need to organize and contest the Church's conservatism. In 1982, they formed *Femmes et ministères* [Women and Ministry] to mobilize women in the Church. One of their first goals was to raise consciousness among

Church women, many of whom believed that feminism was not their concern. Femmes et ministères conducted a broad survey to convince them otherwise. Entitled *Les soutanes roses* [Pink Cassocks], the report created a stir with its long list of discriminatory practices against women in the Church. It was now up to the bishops to respond.

In 1986, the social affairs committee of Québec's Assemblée des évêques [Assembly of Bishops] created an ad hoc committee charged with organizing a major two-day meeting during which the bishops were to deal with issues of concern to feminists. The women planned the meeting very carefully. The bishops were seated amongst 100 women guests and had to listen to what for them were deeply disturbing presentations about power and family, language and employment, sexuality and violence. Symbolically, a woman delivered the homily for the celebration of the Eucharist. During the Words of Consecration, women in the audience spoke the text at the same time as the priest. Traditionally, only the priest was entitled to say those words. Women served communion to the bishops. The meeting ended with a series of practical recommendations, in particular, about the salaries of women who worked for the Catholic Church. A male journalist described the meeting as "the bishops in the lion's den."

Subsequently, panels were organized in the dioceses concerning the partnership of men and women in the Catholic Church, sexuality, and domestic violence. As the priests attending these panels learned, the existing pastoral guidelines needed to be changed. Women would no longer be counselled to offer their sorrows to Christ. In 1989, the Assemblée des évêques published *La violence en heritage: Réflexion pastorale sur la violence conjugale* [Heritage of Violence: Pastoral Reflection on Domestic Violence]. This booklet was further proof of the impact of feminism on all sectors of society.

How strange that the media of the day were fostering the idea that feminism was dying, that feminism had gone too far, or that it was the post-feminist era. Just the opposite was true. Women's groups had never been so numerous or organized, living proof of the essential need for feminism.

Who was right, the media or the feminists? Was feminism out of date?

CHAPTER 29

Feminism Lightens Up

AS THE QUÉBEC-WIDE associations were forming and new groups were mobilizing, the tone of feminism began to lighten. In 1978 the revue *Pluri-elles* changed its name to *Des luttes et des rires de femmes*. The word *rires* [laughter] in the title reflected a desire to change the tone of feminism. But readers still didn't laugh very often. Many women believed that feminists had only bad news to tell and treated all women as victims. They saw the feminist press as too pessimistic and were not very enthusiastic about reading their publications. Then, in 1980, a new magazine was born, at first in the form of an insert in the leftist magazine *Le Temps fou* [Crazy Times]. On the cover was Pope John-Paul II himself, wearing lipstick and announcing the first issue of *La Vie en rose*.

The new magazine featured a livelier and more informal writing style and an attractive layout. "A magazine covering current events from a feminist perspective that will counter the boring psychologizing and sickly optimism of the so-called women's press," asserted *La Vie en rose's* writers, who wanted to break with the "feminist tone" of the 1970s. "A magazine that will offer an alternative to a moralistic, ghettoizing and prudish brand of feminism."

After a year, the magazine came out every other month with a print run of 10,000 per issue. The editorial team, made up mostly from the *Comité de lutte pour l'avortement libre et gratuity*, including Sylvie Dupont, Ariane Émond, Françoise Guénette, Lise Moisan and Francine Pelletier, set compelling goals: to provoke discussion within the feminist movement; to denounce women's oppression; to provide entertainment to women readers; to illustrate the vitality of women's culture. The magazine was punchy and incisive with its saucy tone, eye-catching cover pages, and penchant for controversial

From 1980 to 1987, a cheeky magazine, *La vie en rose*, changed the tone of feminist writing. Here is the first cover featuring Pope Jean-Paul II sporting red lipstick.

issues such as pornography, censorship, the family, housework, the media, love, terrorism, eroticism, and prostitution.

The interviews with feminist notables were legendary: Simone de Beauvoir, Kate Millett, and Benoîte Groult. The interviewers brazenly asked, "Do we like men?" One issue featured erotic stories. In every issue, readers were treated to Andrée Brochu's hilarious cartoons and Hélène Pednault's irreverent columns. In 1985, the magazine switched to monthly publication and doubled its circulation to 20,000 reaching a readership of over 60,000. For March 8, 1984, the writers organized a gigantic party, Rose Tango; 3,500 women showed up.

But eventually the editorial team reached the point of collective burnout. The magazine stopped publication in 1987, despite a circulation of 40,000. Such an enterprise could not survive without advertising and major advertisers wanted nothing to do with *La Vie en rose*. In addition, the editorial team was concerned that women were becoming too individualistic and the members of the collective

ENFIN DUCHESSES!

EN REPRISE AU THÉÂTRE DE QUAT'SOUS
100 avenue des Pins Est • Du 4 mai au 5 juin (20 h)

À Québec du 18 janvier au 5 février
Théâtre de la Bordée
1091 1/2, rue Saint-Jean

À Montréal du 1ᵉʳ au 19 mars
Théâtre expérimental des femmes
320, rue Notre Dame est

were tired. Twenty-five years later, Françoise Guénette confided, "We went off to tend to our private lives, worn out from the zealousness and long hours of the earlier years." All the same, the revue survived nearly eight years, a record for the feminist press.

Established almost at the same time as *La Vie en rose*, the performance company *Les Folles Alliées* [Mad Sisters] appeared in Québec City in the early 1980s. *Les Folles Alliées* was an incredible venture, involving multitalented women performers who practically invented feminist humour in Québec with shows that had an entire generation of women and men rolling in the aisles. Supporters of feminist causes, they described themselves as "racers in a huge relay race."

They wrote a dozen shows in the space of ten years. Three shows toured across Québec. No one who saw them can forget *Enfin duchesses!* which denounced the exploitation of women by the organizers of the winter carnival in Québec City; or *Mademoiselle Autobody* on pornography; or *C'est parti mon sushi ! Un show crû,*

Enfin Duchesses! From 1981 to 1989, a group of female comedians from Québec City, *Les Folles Alliées*, produced numerous feminist humour shows. Multitalented artists, they sang, danced, acted and performed as clowns.

Les Folles Alliées—Spectrum.

which opened with an appearance of the Virgin Mary.

This show had an electroshock effect, revealing male oppression in its rawest details.

Prends-le pas personnel. Prends-le historique! [Take it historically, not personally!]: The Folles Alliées bequeathed to us this retort to men who are uncomfortable around feminists. After ten years the Folles Alliées had to stop due to lack of funding, even though their shows were always sold out.

Other feminist cultural events continued to attract attention. Artists were interested in making films, especially videos, and festivals and groups organized countless exhibitions. Women at the National Film Board continued to produce feminist documentaries. New feminist plays opened in the theatres. Pol Pelletier, an actor, playwright and director, quickly showed herself to be an artist as intense as she was uncompromising.

In just a few years, women artists were expressing themselves in paintings, choreography, character sketches, photographs, installations and writing. They broke new ground. Women were no longer simply the objects of male artists' gaze. They protested the essentially male tradition that predominated in all the art forms.

One event in particular caught the public's attention. In the winter of 1982, the exhibition known as *The Dinner Party*, by U.S. artist Judy Chicago, arrived in Montréal. An enormous triangular table was set with 39 places for notable women in world history, each of them represented by a plate adorned with a stylized depiction of the female vulva. At the centre of the space created by the 39 place settings, the names of hundreds of women were inscribed on white tiles. It was a powerful piece. In an adjoining room where the crowd filed by, two local works were on display, *La Chambre nuptiale* by Francine Larivée and a huge quilt created by women from every region of Québec.

For most of those who visited the exhibition, it was a genuine consciousness-raising experience. However, some men disapproved. One intellectual protested: "You can't make activist art!" Comments such as this reveal the double standard women artists faced. Activist art has a long male history. Wasn't Picasso's *Guernica* a political painting?

During the 1980s the feminist message persisted, always bold and incisive. But the brightness of the preceding decade had faded. A current of opposition, at first tentative, then steadily more overt, began to emerge against feminist analysis and the actions of the women's movement. As in the early 20th century, anti-feminist attacks became pervasive.

How did this anti-feminism manifest itself?

CHAPTER 30

Mounting Anti-Feminism

SINCE ITS APPEARANCE in Québec at the end of the 19th century, the feminist movement has generated hostility. Opposition came from journalists like Henri Bourassa (founder of *Le Devoir* known for his anti-women's suffrage editorials in the 1910s), politicians like Alexandre Taschereau (Québec premier who defeated women's suffrage bill in the 1920s), and bishops like Cardinal Villeneuve (opposed women's suffrage and nurses' unionization in the 1930s). We could fill another book with all the anti-feminist opinions that have been expressed. This opposition has always blocked any change to the social order. They were against women's suffrage; against equal rights under the *Civil Code*; against married women in the labour market; against equal pay for women; against girls' access to higher education; against women's presence in politics; against daycare; against birth control; against women's right to abortion. Anti-feminism is also fed by an age-old tradition of misogyny, hatred and contempt for women, which dates from the beginnings of patriarchy. In the United States, during the 1980s, people began talking about the anti-feminist "backlash," a backlash that was also felt in Québec.

By the end of the 20th century, anti-feminist attacks were taking a different form, because feminist victories had significantly changed the status quo. Most people acknowledged that feminists' demands made sense. As one male journalist commented: "They [the feminists] are undeniably right. There's nothing wrong with what they're saying and their goals."

Yet, the changes disturbed many men who did not want to lose the advantages they enjoyed as males in a society where women had yet to attain full equality. Many men were extremely reluctant to accept women's autonomy. Meanwhile, a lot of women who were only too happy to benefit from the new possibilities open to them, considered that feminism was no longer necessary. In many workplaces, including legal firms, the media, and the business world, it was not in a woman's interest to express feminist ideas.

THE ANTI-FEMINISM OF *L'ACTUALITÉ*

A popular magazine, *L'Actualité* (the equivalent of *Maclean's* in Québec and published since 1976), covered feminism in Québec in a completely distorted and inaccurate manner. According to *L'Actualité*, feminism was only ten years old in 1978 and 20 years old six years later, in 1984. Feminism had existed in Québec since 1893, but no one seemed to know it. In April 1984, *L'Actualité* proclaimed that men now felt useless and were suffering from the "worker bee or drone syndrome."

"Men are silent because they're afraid no one will understand them."

"Feminism has killed romance and desire."

"Feminism has caused profound upheaval."

"Feminism is hypocritical."

When the magazine did address a feminist issue, it always referred to the situation in the United States or in France. There was never a word about the actions or initiatives of feminists in Québec, an effective way of diminishing their political significance. *L'Actualité* regularly announced the imminent death of feminism: "It makes sense that feminism should now take a back seat." It never missed an opportunity to say that while Québec women were happy to benefit from feminists' victories, none of them wanted to be defined as a feminist.

Radio hotlines echoed anti-feminist sentiments with comments such as, "Women have no business driving school buses."

THE WOMEN'S PRESS

Advertisers forced women's magazines, *Châtelaine* and many others, to stop promoting feminist ideas. The magazines adopted the new language, using words like "freedom," "independence," and "equality," but using them in the context of frivolous articles on how to choose your make-up, fashion, therapy, psychological tests, and dieting. All this was presented in a package that featured half-naked nymphets in suggestive poses. It was impossible to leaf through *Châtelaine* and not feel old, ugly, and badly dressed, even when you knew that the photos had been airbrushed. An activist from the women's health centre declared, "Women's magazines have become dangerous to women's health."

A female *Châtelaine* executive deflected the criticism, "Today, feminism is much less about talk, it's about action. We at *Châtelaine* intend to focus on work, careers, and finances. We cannot impose such a categorical perspective on all our readers." Yet, *Châtelaine* had no problem reducing the image of femininity to plastic surgery, silicone breasts, and lace underwear. The cult of beauty at any price constituted the most insidious aspect of anti-feminism.

In a TV interview on feminism, a women's magazine editor responded: "Oh! Feminism is so old hat!" People no longer wanted to hear from feminists. "What do feminists do? They yell a lot. Why don't you just shut up? You're going to wreck everything." suggested a prominent sovereigntist and journalist, Pierre Bourgault, in 1986.

ABORTION IN THE HEADLINES AGAIN

And yet, the struggles of the preceding decade were far from over. Abortion was still making headlines. In several regions, a huge outcry greeted efforts to get rid of the hospital committees that had been set up to review women's requests for therapeutic abortions. In 1989, only 12 out of 168 community health clinics and 35 out of 140 hospitals offered abortion services.

Parti Québécois MNA, Jean-Yves Mercier, spoke out publicly "on nationalist grounds" against publicly funded abortion clinics. He was supported by a group called *Combat pour la vie* [Fight for Life] that was led by a former boxing star named Reggie Chartrand who had published a book in 1984 called *Dieu est un homme parce qu'il est bon et fort. La révolte d'un homme contre le féminisme* [God is a man because he is good and he is strong. One Man's Revolt against Feminism]. This book was one long list of quotations from male authors through the centuries, from Aristotle to Woody Allen, each of them denigrating women. The book enjoyed a brief *succès de scandale*.

In 1985, Reggie Chartrand sued Dr. Morgentaler. The judge decided that Chartrand's lawsuit was "frivolous and vexatious." The next year Chartrand sued another physician, setting off a long legal saga. In the latter case, the chief of police of the city of Trois-Rivières blamed women who chose to terminate their pregnancy saying: "They are cruel and murderous females."

Activists rose up and demanded a public apology, but the municipal council defended its police chief, quoting Québec's *Charte des droits et libertés*.

In 1988, the Supreme Court of Canada struck down the provisions of the *Criminal Code* concerning abortion so that abortion was no longer a crime. Would women who needed an abortion finally be free of the legal obstacles?

In the summer of 1989, the Chantal Daigle case exploded into public consciousness. The young woman at the centre of the case was trapped in an abusive relationship with her boyfriend, Jean-Guy Tremblay. When she became pregnant, he became more and more violent, controlling her every move. She left him and decided

As a 21 year old woman from Val d'Or, Chantal Daigle fled an abusive relationship. Her boyfriend obtained an injunction from the Québec courts preventing her from having an abortion. She appealed to the Supreme Court of Canada which, on November 16, 1989, ruled that the father had no legal right to control the mother or her foetus.

to have an abortion. At that point, he obtained an injunction from the Québec Superior Court prohibiting Daigle from getting an abortion. This was a first in Québec. Chantal Daigle decided to fight the injunction; and she had to fight it all the way up to the Supreme Court of Canada. The case was extensively covered by the media and the pro-life and pro-choice camps rose up in force. Feminists in the Coalition québécoise pour le droit à l'avortement libre et gratuit organized huge demonstrations. Over 10,000 people, mostly women, hit the streets to support Chantal Daigle. On July 27, 1989, women read out the *Manifeste des femmes du Québec* in five different languages, a passionate defence of women's right to abortion:

> The scope of this judgment is extremely grave for women. This judgment has just handed men, boyfriends, husbands, the power to individually control women's freedom and reproductive lives. This is a patriarchal decision in the true meaning of the term. It gives fathers more power than mothers over maternity. It uses the notion of the foetus' right to life to reinforce male power.

With her pregnancy advancing, the slowness of the legal process was a huge threat for Chantal Daigle. She could no longer wait. Assisted by activists from the Centre de santé des femmes de Montréal, she left for Boston on July 30, 1989, to have the abortion. She was disguised as a punk, with red and green hair, and accompanied by her mother. A few days after her return, the Supreme Court of Canada released its decision: The injunction against her was lifted. The judgment was clear:

> The foetus is not included in the term "human being" in the *Québec Charter* or a "person" under the *Canadian Charter of Rights and Freedoms*... No Court in Québec or elsewhere has ever accepted the argument that a father's interest in a foetus, which he has helped create, could support his right to veto a woman's decisions in respect of the foetus she is carrying. A number of cases in various jurisdictions outside of Québec have considered this argument and explicitly rejected it. ... This lack of a legal basis is fatal to the argument about "fathers' rights."

Chantal Daigle returned to private life, while her former boyfriend continued making headlines for his violence against a succession of new partners.

THE MASSACRE AT ÉCOLE POLYTECHNIQUE

On December 6, 1989, a young man walked into the Université de Montréal's École polytechnique. Armed with an automatic weapon, he calmly entered classrooms, separated the young women from the young men and systematically shot the women.

"You're all just a bunch of feminists!" he yelled.

"We're not feminists. We're just women who want to be engineers," one woman protested.

In a matter of minutes, he had killed 14 women and wounded 13 others. He then turned his weapon on himself and fired, killing himself. This horrible event was covered by media around the world.

Women immediately understood the meaning of his act: hatred of feminists had provoked his murderous rampage. He shouted it out as he went from one classroom to the next. He wrote it in a letter that was later found among his belongings: "Even though the media will label me as a CRAZED GUNMAN, I believe that I'm a rational and educated person. Feminists have always known how to infuriate me." There was also a list of names of well-known women he wanted to assassinate.

The message could not have been more clear. Yet initially, the authorities would only release the list of women targets. The text of the letter was withheld to hide the political significance of his action. "I offer my sincere condolences to the families of the dead students," education minister Claude Ryan said on television (using the male or neutral French word for students). But Mr. Ryan, all of those students were WOMEN. Why refuse to admit it?

In the hallways of Radio-Canada journalist Francine Pelletier heard the comment "He should have killed them all!"

Feminists found themselves muzzled from speaking out. The political significance of the crime was a forbidden topic. Feminist articles and letters to the newspapers were not published. He had killed young women training to be engineers, because he considered them to be feminists—and yet no one was allowed to say that. As

Les Folles Alliées stated, "We know from a very good source that our anger is not only frowned on, it is a prohibited emotion."

"Feminists are trying to co-opt a news story" was the common refrain. But, while feminist expertise was prohibited, "psychological" interpretations were rolled out with nauseating frequency. "I'm amazed there haven't been more incidents like this," a physician calmly remarked in a TV interview.

This episode marked the beginning of an explicit and virulent wave of anti-feminism. A year later, journalist Roch Côté published his *Manifeste d'un salaud* [Manifesto of a Bastard], in which he questioned and ridiculed the statistics on violence against women.

"Next to these exaggerated texts on violence against women, the Battle of Stalingrad could be described as the 'the Red Army's Holiday.'"

Feminists were dismayed by Roch Côté's pamphlet. But many men had a different response: "I experienced Roch Côté's *Manifeste d'un salaud* as liberating," admitted journalist Louis Cornellier in 2007, who had been a student at the time of the massacre.

How would the anti-feminist forces affect the women's movement?

CHAPTER 31

Galvanizing Women

THE TRAGEDY OF École Polytechnique and the reactions of the media, opinion leaders and so called 'experts' had a galvanizing effect on feminists. In no time, feminists threw themselves into several major projects: the celebration of the 50th anniversary of women obtaining the vote, participation in the Canadian constitutional debate following the failure of the Meech Lake Accord, and the organization of a symposium to define a feminist vision of society.

While this chapter will focus on these three events, it is important to remember that, at the same time, thousands of women continued to work in the hundreds of centres that had been set up during the previous two decades. Those who were upset by all this activity thought women had gone too far. The demise of feminism had been proclaimed since 1976, right after International Women's Year. "Masculinist" or fathers' rights groups began to pop up to protest against this enduring feminist presence.

THE 50TH ANNIVERSARY OF WOMEN'S RIGHT TO VOTE

The anniversary of women's right to vote was the ideal opportunity for a status report. The process started with a gigantic consultation with all women's groups called *Et si on se racontait le féminisme* [What if we talked about feminism]. It was a fantastic collective undertaking which, though a little rocky at times, ended up a huge success. The Groupe des 13 played a significant role and was joined by other associations such as the Cercles de fermières (despite their aim to remain independent and their reluctance to endorse feminist goals). In the spring of 1990, the result was published in the form of a book dedicated to the two groups:

To our true mothers, most of them hidden behind our

fathers' names, and to our other mothers, the Marie Lacoste-Gérin-Lajoies, Thérèse Casgrains, and Idola Saint-Jeans, activists who won the right to vote for all of us and in so doing, tore a few holes in the walls of patriarchy.

To our daughters, who, freed of their mothers' bitterness, can take this beautiful and challenging story of the efforts and struggles of women in Québec and walk proudly, perhaps even joyously, toward a future where they will inevitably be tasked with investing *en masse* for the survival of the planet.

The following paragraph, a reference to the 1989 École Polytechnique massacre, was included in the dedication to provide contemporary context:

> After the tragic event which during those cold and dark days of December 1989, smashed down like a huge and devastating blast, every women's group was seized with fear, horror, and despair. The days went by, one day following another. We got back up. Once again, much courage was needed to rekindle the flame of hope.

The organizers of the 50th anniversary of women's right to vote called the celebration *Femmes en tête* (with its double meaning, "women in the lead" and "women in mind"). Women's groups in every region organized theatrical performances, forums, and panels that brought hundreds of women together. It concluded with a huge three-day gathering in Montréal called *Les 50 heures du féminisme*. Lise Payette was asked to be the honorary president of the event.

However, a few months earlier, Lise Payette had produced a television documentary entitled *Disparaître* [Disappearing] about Québec's declining birth rate and the menace posed by the increasing number of immigrants. The documentary angered the cultural communities, resulting in the Association des femmes immigrantes' decision to boycott *Femmes en tête*. In the end, the event took place anyway. The women's centres of l'R des centres de femmes seized the occasion to protest the federal government's recent funding cuts by unfurling dozens of banners inside the atrium of the Université du Québec à Montréal while the speakers were addressing the crowd on the first evening of the event. The effect was spectacular. Women

LES 50 HEURES DU FÉMINISME

1 9 4 0

forum-prospectives
réservé aux femmes

27, 28, 29 avril 1990

50^e

1 9 9 0

femmes en tête

U.Q.A.M.
université du québec à montréal

La Presse   CKAC 73   billets en vente dans tous les comptoirs Ticketron.
Télétron : 288-2525

then spent the next two days in a host of workshops, discussing feminist issues.

For the closing event on April 28, 1990, everyone gathered at the Maurice Richard Arena for a grand production, directed by the famous theatre, film, and television actress, Denise Filiatrault. The evening started with a short play recounting the steps in the saga of winning the vote: *L'incroyable histoire de la lutte que quelques-unes ont menée pour obtenir le droit de vote pour toutes* [The incredible story of a few women's struggle to win the vote for the rest of us]. The audience was then treated to a show featuring a wonderful line-up of enthusiastic performers. The atmosphere was electric. Women departed bursting with energy to continue the struggle. In a nearby Metro station, hundreds of women waited on both sides of the platform. When the train arrived in the station and they saw that a woman was driving, she was applauded like a heroine, a symbol of a century's worth of women's victories.

For the 50th anniversary of the women's vote in Québec, Denise Filiatrault directed a memorable show featuring enthusiastic performers including Pauline Julien, Clémence DesRochers, and Margie Gillis.

Around the same time, the Assemblée des évêques held an event that was almost as spectacular, but much less noticed by feminists. In Québec City's Cathedral, the bishops gathered to make amends for opposing women's suffrage for so long and thereby depriving women of their fundamental rights. Did this mean that the demands of Christian feminists would now be heard? That would have been a stretch! Numerous women refused to attend the ceremony, because they were not interested in endorsing a gesture that, in the end, did not commit the bishops to making any significant change. One feminist theologian decided to go, dressed in black and wearing a hat and antique jewellery. As she explained, "I decided to accept the bishops' apology as a gesture of reparation to my mother and all the women of her generation who were oppressed by the Church."

Meanwhile, Rome issued several restrictive edicts on the role of women in the Church. The Catholic Church in Québec, reputedly one of the most liberal in the Christian world, slowly got back in line. After all, the bishops had to obey orders from Rome.

The media response to the anniversary events was predictably bland. Still not convinced that feminism was alive and well, mocking journalists continued to file colourless stories to their papers. When *La Presse* published a special insert on feminism to mark the anniversary of women's suffrage, a male journalist protested, "How do you justify a special section, as if we were at a turning point in history? No. It's just the anniversary of women's right to vote."

FEMINISTS AND THE CONSTITUTIONAL DEBATE

Meanwhile, journalists were writing tirelessly and vigorously about the constitutional debates underway during the same period. Feminists were present, but the general public heard nothing about this. Since the 1980 referendum debate that had polarized feminists, women's ideas and roles in society had evolved. Having just celebrated the 50th anniversary of women's suffrage, feminists wanted to continue the tradition and play an active role in the constitutional debate.

When the Constitution was patriated in 1982, the federal government's unilateral action had angered many Québecers and worried feminists. Many of them believed that women were mostly absent from the constitutional debate and that "if there were another Constitution, it was more than likely that it would once again reflect the consensus of a bunch of new fathers of Confederation."

But feminists were not unanimous in their views on the national question. In 1987, when the public was invited to take a position on the Meech Lake Accord that the Mulroney government had concluded with the provinces, the Fédération des femmes du Québec presented a brief. In their eyes, sexual equality was part of Québec's political culture, essential to Québec as a "distinct society." Meanwhile, English-speaking Canadian feminists attending a pan-Canadian convention declared, "The distinct society clause is a menace to women's rights." The FFQ leaders believed that these feminists were behind the times: "In fact, the progress we have made on women's equality is tied to the concept of distinct society."

In 1990, all eyes were on Ottawa. The provincial premiers were meeting to discuss the ratification of the Meech Lake Accord that would finally allow Québec to sign the Canadian Constitution that had been patriated without its agreement in 1981. The suspense was finally broken when the Accord failed, leading to the creation of the Bloc Québécois, a new federal party that women joined in droves.

The failure of the Meech Accord led the Québec government, then headed by Robert Bourassa's Liberal Party, to set up a major commission on the constitutional status of Québec, the Bélanger-Campeau Commission. Nearly all the organizations in Québec were invited to sit on the commission, with the exception of women's groups. Feminists protested.

Union leader Lorraine Page, a member of the Commission representing the teacher's labour central (CEQ), commented: "Women were told we were over-reacting, that women's opinions would be amply represented and taken into account. It was also pointed out that, as a woman, trade unionist, teacher, and feminist, I could easily 'play this role.' Of course I wouldn't get to speak four times as often as my co-commissioners, but it would seem that the double, triple and even quadruple day applies to parliamentary commissions too!"

The Fédération des femmes du Québec presented a brief that

was openly sovereigntist while not endorsing a particular political party. Feminists understood the importance of autonomy and identity. These issues have always been at the heart of the women's movement. If women wanted a feminist vision of society for Québec, then Québec must be able to control the means to ensure its full development.

Nearly 20 women's groups presented briefs to the commissioners. Much energy was devoted to preparing these documents. Women were determined that their voices be heard. But it quickly became clear that economic concerns would take priority over everything else. In the final report, women's concerns were barely touched. A tiny paragraph in the conclusion refers to the principle of sexual equality. "If we hadn't said anything, the result would have been the same" feminists raged.

In the wake of their participation in these key political debates, many feminists believed that it was important for women to define what kind of society they wanted to build, even before posing the question of Québec independence. This is why the FFQ launched a new forum, inviting its members to collectively define a feminist vision of society. Women were invited to a huge gathering (yet another one) to discuss their vision. The result was an innovative document entitled *Pour un Québec féminin pluriel* [For A Feminist Pluralist Québec] that set out the kind of society in which women wanted to live.

The years from 1989 to 1993 were tumultuous and difficult for the FFQ, with the resignation of a president, administrative problems, the cessation of the newsletter, and funding cutbacks. It is remarkable that they were able to initiate so much political activity during this period. The FFQ was surviving on the efforts of a few volunteers, in particular, the Conseil général de Montréal. Feminist activism had been transferred to a new generation of activists.

WALKING THE HALLS OF POWER

Meanwhile, women were becoming more visible in the spheres of power. Québec women were entering politics in ever increasing numbers and were members of all the political parties. In 1990, there were 23 women members (MNAs) in Québec's National Assembly, while only 13 women were sitting in the House of Commons. But how successful were they in breaking down the last bastions of male power? It soon became clear that even if the proportion of elected women had increased in Parliament as well as in other decision-making spheres, it levelled off at 30 per cent.

When women voted for the first time in the Montréal municipal election of 1904, Marie Gérin-Lajoie wrote in her diary, "We've broken the ice and I believe we will never go back." The ice had been broken, certainly, but it came back in another form, at the top of organizations and institutions: the glass ceiling.

This is why, in the mid 1990s, women across Québec formed groups to encourage women to enter politics. In Ottawa, former and currently serving women MPs mentored new women candidates. But most women were interested in municipal politics because it was much closer to home. Many women held very senior positions in Montréal, for example. They felt they were in the right place at the right time.

One of the support groups for women in politics, *Pépines*, was founded in 1992 in Sherbrooke. They were dedicated to promoting women's role at all levels of decision-making. The halls of power throughout Estrie (formerly called the Eastern Townships) now had to contend with the Pépines. They publicized a list of women who were ready to take decision-making positions. They demanded women's presence in positions of power. They honoured anyone, male or female, who encouraged social equity. They organized information sessions on controversial public debates.

Similar groups appeared throughout Québec: *Groupe Femmes, politique et démocratie* [Women, Politics, and Democracy], *Réseau des élues municipales de la Montérégie* [Montérégie Women's Network of Elected Officials], *Femmes et politique municipale de l'Estrie* [Women and Municipal Politics in Estrie], *Femmes d'influence de Lévis* [Influential Women of Lévis)] and many others. They were effective. The proportion of women mayors rose from 1.3 per cent in 1980 to 13 per cent in 2005. The proportion of women city counsellors rose from 3 per cent in 1980 to 27 per cent in 2005. Soon, women's committees appeared in the Union of Municipalities of Québec and the Québec Federation of Municipalities. Direct political involvement rapidly became a new and dynamic aspect of the feminist movement. After 2000, these women organized seminars for future candidates to prepare them for political life. These organizations demonstrated that women and power were compatible.

Nevertheless, the position of feminists remained uncertain. Women had their foot in the door, but for many feminists it was not enough to be like men. Would women be able to transform power or would power transform women? For example, feminists debated whether the fact that women could now join the armed forces was a feminist victory. Some regretted that pacifism did not play a more significant role in feminist action. And still others believed that feminism did not take "ordinary women" sufficiently into account.

Was there a way to unite feminists in collective action?

CHAPTER 32

A New Wave of Organizing

PARADOXICALLY, THE 1990s were marked by the absence of young feminists. Young women at CÉGEPs [junior colleges] and in the job market did not identify at all with the feminist movement; they considered it outdated. They felt that they could do and be whatever they wanted to do and be, so why wouldn't anyone else have been able to do the same? They were much like the young women of the 1960s who had no interest in women's organizations.

"The word 'feminism' makes people nervous" some young women said. "That was a movement for the older generation. They were really into it and then they got tired of it. Maybe it made sense for them at the time, but it doesn't interest me."

Young women found feminists too radical and too aggressive. They wanted to work and collaborate with men. Some commented, "Maybe we would be more interested in feminism if men were involved too."

They were in favour of the gains feminists had made, women's freedom, and women's independence. They denounced sexism as it still existed and wanted more equal relationships with men. Their standards for a future partner were very high. Young women said: "If I had to choose between having children and a spouse, I'd choose just to have the kids."

Responses to a survey in Québec in 1992 showed strong support (over 85 per cent) for feminist gains such as equality and pay equity; shared housework and childrearing; daycare; work-family balance; women's access to political life and senior management positions; and the demedicalization of childbirth. Support was weakest for birth control, especially abortion, but even so, it stood at 70 per cent. Lastly, 22 per cent of those surveyed described themselves as "definitely feminist" and 29 per cent as "probably feminist." Was the support of half the population enough to change the world? It was increasingly clear that, in the 1990s, society's big challenge was to adjust to women's expanded roles.

THE FÉDÉRATION DES FEMMES DU QUÉBEC UNDERGOES A TRANSFORMATION

After the large gatherings of the early 1990s—*Les 50 heures du féminisme*, *Un Québec féminin pluriel*—new issues emerged. Many activists in the FFQ, especially its individual members, were convinced that the FFQ represented all women. They wanted the FFQ to continue functioning as it had for over 25 years.

The women who worked on the front lines saw things differently. Every day, they met women who were confronted with multiple problems, but were not necessarily interested in feminist theory. Feminists who provided services to women often had a different vision of feminism, one that was closer to the reality of their clients, many of whom had been left behind by the feminist revolution. Since these activists were now members of the FFQ, their influence began to be felt at the annual conventions and was a factor in the important repositioning of this key organization.

The FFQ's traditional way of working was challenged at its 1994 annual meeting by women who wanted to give more power to the increasing number of group members. They wanted to reduce the influence of individual members, accept new categories of members, include the regional women's coalitions, and reach out to groups representing women with multiple forms of oppression, including lesbians, Aboriginal women, immigrants, and women with disabilities. "A wind of change is blowing over the FFQ," declared a female journalist in 1994.

At that time, most individual FFQ members were paid employees working for the women's movement. Many long-time activists, among them women in the regional councils who had tirelessly volunteered to keep the FFQ going for over a quarter century, felt maligned and quit the Fédération. This was the situation when Françoise David, then coordinator of l'R des centres de femmes, assumed the role of FFQ president. She replaced Céline Signori, who had decided to run for the Parti Québécois in the 1994 election.

Françoise David, President of the Fédération des femmes du Québec (1994-2001), was one of the women responsible for the 1995 Du pain et des roses march and the 2000 World March of Women against Poverty and Violence.

Françoise David brought to the feminist movement a focus that was directed at women's economic problems. Her work in leftist groups during the 1970s had shaped her vision of feminism. In her personal evolution as an activist, it had taken a while before she had incorporated a feminist analysis. She was very enthusiastic about one of the FFQ's projects, an anti-poverty march, but was firm about one point: "It's not a march against women's poverty; it's a women's march against poverty."

BREAD AND ROSES MARCH

Françoise David began a Québec-wide tour to persuade women's groups to participate in a project that would involve walking 200 kilometres, housing and feeding 150 women, mobilizing over 10,000 women, and drafting clear and achievable demands from the government. It was quickly decided that the march would be called *Du pain et des roses* [Bread and Roses]. The title came from a long time organizing tradition for women. In 1912, in New York City, a striking woman worker had held a picket sign reading, "We want bread, but we want roses too!" The slogan reappeared over the years in countless other demonstrations. Almost immediately the Du pain

Women's March, *Du pain et des roses*. In 1995 feminists mobilized across Québec in a march to sensitize the public and the government about poverty.

et des roses march sparked public interest and support. Better yet, the media was sympathetic.

On May 26, 1995, hundreds of women started marching toward Québec City. They left Montréal and followed the north shore of the St. Lawrence River. They left Longueuil (the south shore across the river from Montréal) and marched through the regions of Montérégie, Estrie and the Centre du Québec. They left Rivière-du-Loup (the lower St. Lawrence valley) and marched up the south shore of the St. Lawrence. In every city or town they passed, local feminists walked with them, sheltered them, and offered support. On June 4, the three contingents converged in front of the National Assembly in Québec City to present their demands to Premier Jacques Parizeau. A crowd

of nearly 20,000 awaited them, cheering and singing the march's theme song, "Du pain et des roses, pour changer les choses!" [Give us bread and roses and we'll make changes.]

Despite its small budget, the march had a huge public impact. The list of demands was very concrete: a system for the automatic deduction of child support payments; a tuition freeze and larger student bursaries; the creation of 1,500 new social housing units per year; access for all women to basic education and occupational training services and programs, accompanied by adequate financial assistance with a view to labour market integration; a social infrastructure program with jobs for women; reduction from ten to three years of sponsorship for immigrant women sponsored by a husband; access to social programs for immigrant women who were victims of domestic and family violence; pay equity legislation; and an increase in the minimum wage.

In the years that followed, many of these demands were met, thanks to the persistence of feminists, pressure on the government, and the collaboration of women in all political parties sitting in the National Assembly, especially during the passage of the *Pay Equity Bill* in 1996.

WOMEN'S GATHERING IN BEIJING

At the end of the summer of 1995, a number of feminists from Québec went to Beijing, China for the United Nations' 4th World Conference on Women, following the Nairobi Conference of 1985, the 1980 Conference in Copenhagen, and the 1975 Conference in Mexico City. At the first World Conference in Mexico City, women from Third World countries were relatively silent. Since then, their influence had gradually grown and they were successful in getting their priorities placed on the conference agenda. At the Nairobi Conference of 1985, they made a big impact on western feminists, who returned home convinced that western solutions could not necessarily be applied in developing countries.

At Beijing, however, grassroots organizations were pushed to the sidelines. The conference was once again dominated by a few white women from the West, notably conservative right-wing women from the U.S. In that sea of delegates from Africa, South America, and Asia, white women had become a visible minority. Yet they were still the ones controlling the UN's institutions. Also present in Beijing were the Catholic, Evangelical and Muslim fundamentalist groups. In the end, the final report was not adopted by all the member states and it was accompanied by dozens of minority declarations that rejected feminist gains.

THE 1995 REFERENDUM

In the fall of 1995, women returned from Beijing to a Québec that was vibrating with the excitement about a new referendum on Québec sovereignty. Would Québec feminists be divided once again and would the "Yvettes" be back in the news? Not at all. The "Yvettes" no longer existed. But, as in 1980, women and feminists were not unanimous in their views on the referendum question. The sovereigntists were the only ones who associated Québec independence with women's independence. The 1970s slogan resurfaced: *Pas de libération des femmes sans libération du Québec. Pas de libération du Québec sans libération des femmes.* [No women's liberation without the liberation of Québec. No liberation of Québec without women's liberation.] In the federalist camp, just as in 1980, women never addressed women's or explicitly feminist concerns during the referendum campaign.

Few women were turning out to the meetings organized by the OUI and NON camps, so a group of sovereigntist women decided to reach out to women by touring around Québec in a bus. There were 44 women coming from every region of Québec, and they called themselves the *Caravane de la souveraineté*, with the fabulous slogan: *Parler à haute voix au lieu de murmurer notre existence* [Speak out instead of whispering our existence].

They drove 4,000 kilometres in 10 days. Feminist groups and women trade unionists welcomed them wherever they went, organizing dinner meetings, theatrical performances, speak-outs, and discussions. Women responded enthusiastically, with a celebration in Estrie, an enormous rally in Longueuil, friendly gatherings in Saguenary and Abitibi, and even a secret meeting on the side of a roadway in the Outaouais, where sovereignty was loathed. At the end of the trek, women gathered for a memorable evening, *Souveraines*, at Club Soda in Montréal, hosted by well-known feminist writer and humourist Hélène Pednault. That night, Pauline Julien, the beloved feminist and sovereigntist singer/performer, appeared for her last time in public.

The amazing result of the referendum, a tiny majority for the NON side (50.58 per cent), ushered in a period of gloom in Québec. In discussions about the social economy, zero deficits, and new global issues, some people were tempted to blame feminists for upsetting the traditional balance in society, provoking change, and raising insoluble problems. Many people said the feminists had gone too far. Such comments reinforced right wing forces and were one example among many manifestations of anti-feminism at the dawn of the new millennium.

Nevertheless, women were eager to relive the excitement of the Du pain et des roses march. Since globalization was a pressing issue, the FFQ proposed a world march of women.

Would Québec feminists succeed in rallying women around the world?

CHAPTER 33

The World March of Women in the Year 2000

IN 1995, FOLLOWING THE successful Du pain et des roses march organized in Québec by the Fédération des femmes du Québec, several FFQ activists, including the president, Françoise David, were in Beijing for the UN's 4ᵗʰ World Conference on Women. They participated in the parallel meetings of non-governmental organizations (NGO) held at the same time as the official sessions of state parties. In the politically charged atmosphere that characterized those NGO meetings, the FFQ women put forth the idea of a march that would bring women together in action.

An international event initiated by the FFQ, the World March of Women in the Year 2000, culminated in October 2001. Some 114 national coordinating bodies organized 50 national marches. Thousands of women marched worldwide.

Women felt the need for a world-wide movement of women at the grassroots level, not just the privileged white experts who controlled the international structures. When they got back to Québec, they sketched out an ambitious proposal: the World March of Women for the Year 2000.

This event mobilized a whole new generation of women. They were no longer the middle-class philanthropists of the first half of the 20ᵗʰ century or the university graduates and professionals of the second half of the 20ᵗʰ century; they were ordinary women and, most importantly, women in countries throughout the world. They successfully rose to a monumental challenge: finding sponsors, organizing preparatory meetings, putting up foreign delegates, preparing documents, organizing publicity, and coordinating the whole event.

This initiative from Québec, which received such an enthusiastic response from women around the globe, was a remarkable achievement. Over 6,000 women's groups from 161 countries mobilized. They set up 114 national coordinating structures and

organized 50 national marches. Between March 8 and October 17, 2000, thousands of women around the world marched. They had meetings with the President of the World Bank, the Managing Director of the International Monetary Fund in Washington, and the Secretary General of the United Nations in New York City. Rather than simply attend a meeting organized by these world leaders, they demanded that the leaders meet with them.

Five years later, in 2005, there was another international action, this time to adopt the *Women's World Charter for Humanity*. It was preceded by a lengthy process to draft, discuss, adopt, and disseminate the Charter. The creation of the Women's World Charter for Humanity signalled the emergence of a new international feminist movement that, inspired by the values of equality, freedom, solidarity, justice, and peace, was bolstered by a comprehensive action plan. The Charter states: "The values [in the Charter] form a whole. They are of equal importance, are interdependent, and indivisible, and the order they appear in the Charter is interchangeable."

This time, millions of women mobilized. They included women who worked on the front lines in the areas of economy, health, violence, and education. A permanent secretariat was set up in Québec in 2001. Later, it moved to Brazil. On March 8, 2005, a relay march left São Paulo, Brazil, with the goal of reaching Ouagadougou, Burkina Faso, in October.

Why did this powerful international movement emerge out of Québec? In the *favelas*, shanty towns, rural regions of Africa, Asian megalopolises, indigenous communities of diverse nations, Québec came to represent a beacon of hope. The fact that Québec had not been a colonizing nation or started any wars was no doubt a factor. Beyond this was the focus that Québec feminists had always placed on the eradication of poverty and violence, issues with which women in developing countries could easily identify. Women from developing countries wanted more than the gender equality discourse spouted by western-dominated international bodies. Feminism was now challenging the founding principles of modern democracy: the notions of freedom, equality, and solidarity would have to be revisited to ensure they included all women.

NEW RADICAL GROUPS

Did these massive feminist projects interest younger women after 2000? Like their 1960s counterparts, many of them believed there were much more important causes to promote. Concerned about the future of the planet, they joined environmental groups. Young women became involved in the anti-globalization movement and joined in the protests at the meetings of international financial bodies. Those who went to developing countries returned appalled by the huge gap between countries of the northern and the southern hemispheres. And they did all these things with young men at their sides.

New radical feminist groups appeared, mainly in Montréal, shortly after 2000. This poster announces the Rassemblement des jeunes féministes [Rally of young feminists] in 2003, organized by the FFQ's youth committee.

New feminist groups began to emerge on university and college campuses. As in the late 1960s, young women challenged the traditional image of femininity. They also criticized the image of feminists. It was the "riot grrrl" era, complete with body piercing, tattoos, and fluorescent hair. They demanded the right to be robust, sexual, and aggressive. More and more, they organized around issues that transcended borders. They knew that feminism confronted global capitalism and patriarchy, and for many of them the feminist movement was most meaningful on an international level.

The young feminists were provocative, as reflected in the names of their groups: *Adieu Capriarcat*, *Sorcières*, *Insoumises*, *Amères Noëlles*, and *the Blood Sisters*. *Les Lucioles* were known for their political videos. Collectives sprang up in universities around feminist studies programs and in the CÉGEPs (junior colleges). A youth committee, the *Comité jeunes de la* FFQ, organized a gathering of young feminists in 2003 entitled *S'unir pour être rebelles* [Unite to be rebels]. They described themselves as radical feminists, like the feminists of the 1970s. They produced forceful social, economic, and political analysis and circulated it in "zines" and DVDs instead of in the feminist magazines of the earlier era.

Several of the new radical feminist groups came out of the anti-globalization movement. This movement was in many ways similar to the leftist groups that rose up in the late 1960s in support of peoples' liberation movements, the disadvantaged, and the fight against capitalism. Like the women who created women's liberation groups in the 1960s and 1970s, many women broke away from the large anti-globalization organizations where they did not feel heard. They created autonomous women's groups to continue work on the same issues from a women's perspective.

In 1999, for example, a movement was formed to protest the Multilateral Agreement on Investment (MAI or, in French, AMI) that would have freed powerful investors from all political interference. This global protest movement resulted in the failure of the MAI agreement in Seattle. The Québec group that belonged to this international movement was called *SalAMI* [*sal* is French for "dirty"] and many young women belonged to it. At first, they organized feminist training workshops. Soon after, in 2000, unhappy with their status in the group, they started a women's committee. Two years later, they withdrew from SalAMI to form *Némésis*. Like the feminists of the 1970s, these feminists were intensely aware of the importance of class and race issues but, since the anti-globalization movements were hesitant to incorporate sexism into their analysis, they had no other choice than to separate from the organizations of men and women and focus on women's equality issues.

At the dawning of the 21th century, what issues would feminists embrace?

In 1997, the FFQ set up a youth committee, Comité jeunes de la FFQ. This put the Federation in contact with the new groups that were springing up everywhere. Many of these young women played a key role in the celebrations for the FFQ's 40th anniversary celebration in 2006.

CHAPTER 34

Contemporary Feminist Debates

YOU WILL RECALL that in the late 1960s, the recently founded Fédération des femmes du Québec was confident that a women's pressure group would succeed in attaining women's demands. To achieve this goal, they pushed for the creation of a Status of Women Council in 1970. That same year, the feminist movement was turned upside down by a burgeoning of women's groups whose members had a radical analysis of what they called "women's oppression." As the list of demands became more extensive, a multitude of feminist services sprang up.

A similar phenomenon has been occurring in recent years. The new generation of feminists do not share certain old school feminist positions that are seen as contemporary manifestations of puritanism. Once again, the feminist agenda is in the midst of transformation, creating splits within the women's movement. Instead of one feminism, it is more accurate to speak of the many "feminisms" that exist today.

This chapter presents an overview of several controversial issues that have shaken up the feminist movement over the past 12 years. This phenomenon is not new. The 20th century had its share of debates that at one time or another pitted feminists against each other: votes for women, women in the paid workforce, wages for housework, abortion, daycare, family inheritance, equal opportunity programs, sexual orientation. In order to change the world, we need to expect and accept differences of opinions.

After gaining the right to control their sexuality and their reproductive lives, women hoped that the sexual double standard would be eradicated. Yet, many questions continue to divide society,

and divide women and feminists. Most often, these divisive issues are connected with women's bodies and sexuality.

Demonstration against pornography

PORNOGRAPHY

In the mid 1990s, the pornography debate resumed, raising a number of new questions. How could it be that feminists, who had historically opposed censorship, were now allying themselves with those seeking to censure pornography? Was this not simply the expression of lingering uneasiness about female sexuality? "Shouldn't women begin producing pornography to express their own sexual fantasies, desires, and choices?" On the other hand, given that pornography is often a teenager's first introduction to *Criticism* sexuality, it is teaching them an essentially violent model of sexuality. *Conclusion*

Divisive questions abound. Isn't Madonna a feminist icon? ✗ Shouldn't we also be fighting for sexual equality in pornography to counter the denigrating representations of women as objects? Does formal equality benefit only a minority of women, leaving the majority, including adolescent girls at the mercy of an invasive pornography industry that encourages violence against women? These are complicated questions to which there are no clear answers and much feminist disagreement.

Stella, a group that works for the rights of women in the sex industry, joined the Fédération des femmes du Québec in 1999. Feminists were deeply divided on the issue of prostitution, but activists with Stella were eager to ally themselves with feminist groups. This photo was taken during an IWD march.

SEX WORKERS

During the "second wave" feminism of the 1970s, prostitutes organized in Lyon, France and Los Angeles, U.S.A. to defend the rights of women in the sex industry, including topless dancers, escorts, and prostitutes. After several attempts, sex workers in Montréal formed an association in 1992. In 1995, a group called *Stella* opened its doors with the goal of improving the working conditions of sex workers. Activists and community workers at Stella denounced the laws on prostitution as criminalizing the practice of a legitimate trade. They challenged the popularly held "whore" stereotypes and developed ways to protect sex workers from HIV and sexually transmitted diseases.

When Stella joined the Fédération des femmes du Québec in 1999, feminists were divided. Many believed that prostitution was essentially harmful to women and should not be considered a job, even when a woman makes this choice. They advocated the abolition of prostitution. A smaller group of feminists believed that prostitution should be legalized. Women should be able to choose this trade. Prostitutes are women who need to be supported, because their struggle is about having the right to be remunerated in exchange for sexual services and doing so in safety and dignity. According to this perspective, prostitution should be decriminalized, but regulated to prevent the exploitation of women who have not chosen to be in the sex industry. Women who are trapped in international sex trafficking, sex tourism, or Internet-based sexual exploitation networks should be protected, while women who choose to participate in sex work should be left alone.

Should prostitution be prohibited or allowed? This question has been an ongoing debate among feminists since the early 1990s, amid a flood of statistics, denunciations, and accusations. On June 18, 2005, two meetings were held in different locations in Montréal. Stella was marking its tenth anniversary, looking back on its years of support, referral, and information services in conjunction with political pressure activities. At the same time, the *Concertation des luttes contre l'exploitation sexuelle* [Coalition Against Sexual Exploitation] was holding its founding meeting to "counter the world-wide discourse that downplays the harm of prostitution and legitimizes the sex industry."

The battle lines have been drawn. At the international level, there are two networks representing the opposing positions: the Coalition Against Trafficking in Women (CATW, 1991), which calls for the abolition of prostitution, and the Global Alliance Against Trafficking in Women (GAATW, 1994), which calls for the decriminalization of all aspects of prostitution based on a personal choice. The intense emotion characterizing this debate speaks to the fragility of an opinion that is attempting to exorcise the antiquated mother/whore dichotomy.

THE HYPERSEXUALIZATION OF GIRLS

In 2000, *Châtelaine* marked its 40th anniversary with a special 300-page issue packed with 162 pages of ads focussed on beauty products and air-brushed glamorous images of very young slender women. This anniversary issue featured a chronology of the magazine's history. The coverage of women's advances during this period was lost in a sea of pointless superficiality. In the middle of the magazine, an emblematic article, *L'ère des Lolitas*, [the Lolita era] addressed the issue of pre-teen girl fashion. The hypersexualization of girls was the most recent prescription for feminine beauty and sexual attractiveness.

"I think the way girls are acting and dressing is very positive. They project a sexy but affirmative image. Yes, they want people to look at them, but it's a statement of self-affirmation, it's not about showing off their bodies. Feminism has brought us forward. Girls are asserting themselves and beginning to own their erotic side," explained a dance instructor.

The contrary was true for many others who argued: "The hypersexualization of girls is a major setback for feminism."

Many women decried the trend of eroticizing little girls, which encourages consumption, increases girls' vulnerability, and is a contemporary way of submitting women to the male gaze. What were mothers thinking when they bought such clothing for their pre-pubescent daughters?

The teenagers themselves were concerned. A young student of 14, Léa Clermont-Dion, spoke out in Montréal in 2006 to warn other girls her age. The media avidly covered all those who denounced the new trend, launched petitions, and had these magazines taken off the news stands.

"It took some consciousness-raising. That was how I got interested in feminism," explained one female high school student.

On the other hand, another teen's response to the groping, stares, and comments inspired by her sexy look was "Hey! What's the problem?" These "sexy" young women are able to wear these clothes *because* they're young. They take advantage of this because they want to feel attractive. But they keep their distance from men who interpret their dress as a message of sexual availability.

This debate heightened in the summer of 2011 with the now famous "Slut Walks," originally organized to protest the 2011 comments of a Toronto police officer who said that if women wanted to be safe on a university campus, they should "not dress like sluts."

In the meantime, hardly anyone notices that it is always the girls who are the targets of criticism about the abuses of fashion trends. No one challenges the boys' behaviour. Not even feminists.

THE ISLAMIC VEIL

The presence of immigrant cultures in Québec has propelled us into debates that we had, until now, believed relevant only in developing countries. Should we accept that many women from these communities wear one of the various forms of headdress prescribed for women: *chador*, *hijab*, even *burka*? There is no consensus among feminists.

Some think traditional head coverings should be tolerated. If it means that girls will be able to pursue their education, we must not impose grounds for excluding them. In 2010, the Fédération des femmes du Québec declared itself in favour of "open secularism," while also respecting the choices of Muslim women. Other feminists believed that religion should be a private matter and that religious symbols should be prohibited in the workplace. In 2011, the Conseil du statut de la femme advocated a rigorous interpretation of secularism as an essential condition of sexual equality.

Meanwhile, a number of Muslim women affirmed their feminist and religious principles. They asked their Québécoise sisters to let them deal with their struggles in their own way, which might include wearing a headscarf. Many women, including some Muslim women, think the veil should be prohibited because it symbolizes male oppression and control of women. Others believe it should be forbidden, because it is a religious symbol and religion has no place in the public sphere. This issue is a complex one, and it is a challenge to think it through.

Yet, it is once again worth noting that it is women's bodies that people want to hide, because of men's "difficulty" in controlling their sexuality, or their assumed rights over women's bodies. In fact, both issues about clothing—teenage girls' hypersexualized presentations and the Islamic headscarf—are two sides of the same coin: the imposition of the male gaze on women, a gaze that women have internalized and turned against themselves. Unquestionably, the sexual double standard that existed a century ago continues as one of the strongest manifestations of patriarchy. As the new radical feminists say, "Women's bodies are still a battlefield."

There is still a lot of feminist work to do. Global issues must not distract us from realizing the fragility of the gains won by feminists in Québec. As feminists, we know that we are at a turning point.

In May 2011, the Fédération des femmes du Québec launched *Les États généraux du féminisme* [the Summit on Feminism], a two-year discussion and review process. Feminists are increasingly reflecting on what they call the "intersectionality" of women's multiple oppressions. All women, white women, Aboriginal women, immigrant women, women belonging to visible minorities, lesbians and transgendered women, and women suffering other forms of exploitation are invited to join in this project. More feminists are realizing that the interests of white middle-class women who have already benefitted from feminism's victories cannot simply be superimposed on the interests of women who are trapped by the combined forces of sexism, racism, and economic exploitation. This raises a daunting question: Is it ever possible to speak on behalf of *all* women?

In the past century, feminism has renewed itself many times, and its players and actions appear to be on the verge of yet another transformation. More than ever, we must count on the young women. And they will be better equipped to act if they know the history of the feminist movement and where to find information that will be indispensable to their cause.

I hope that this short account of feminism and women's history in Québec will be of use to you, my readers.

WORKING TO CHANGE THE WORLD, 1981 TO THE PRESENT

1978   Founding of Réseau des centres d'aide et de lutte contre les agressions à caractère sexuel

1979   Founding of Regroupement des maisons pour femmes victimes de violence conjugale

1980   Launch of *La Vie en rose*

1984   Founding of Conseil d'intervention pour l'accès des femmes au travail (CIAFT)

1985   Founding of Réseau des centres de santé des femmes

        Founding of L'R des centres de femmes du Québec

1986   Founding of Fédération des resources d'hébergement pour femmes en difficulté

1988   Decision of the Supreme Court of Canada in Dr. Henry Morgentaler's case in which abortion was removed from the *Criminal Code*

1989   The Chantal Daigle Case

        The massacre at École Polytechnique

1990   Les 50 heures du féminisme [50th anniversary of women's suffrage]

1992   *Québec féminin pluriel* symposium

1995   La Marche du pain et des roses [Bread and Roses March]

        Referendum on Sovereignty of Québec

2000   World March of Women in the Year 2000

2005   Adoption of the Women's World Charter for Humanity

EPILOGUE

Young Women in 2012

THEIR NAMES ARE Catherine, Stéphanie, Jessica, Audrey, Alexandra, Émilie, Vanessa, Mélanie, Sabrina. They are 17 years old. Almost all of them went to daycare. They're about to enter a CÉGEP. Most plan to go on to university. They're dreaming about holding all kinds of jobs in the future. Nothing is off limits. They know already that, chances are, they won't be getting married, but instead will live in a common-law relationship. Undoubtedly, they will have one or two children later on, once they have established themselves in their careers. They have already been in love and many have had sex.

What do they know about feminism? They were born when women in Québec were celebrating the 50ᵗʰ anniversary of women gaining the vote. They were five at the time of the Du pain et des roses march. They were ten during the World March of Women in the Year 2000. They think that life as it is today happened spontaneously like computers, iPads, and DVDs. The doors to education are open to them. They can prepare themselves for almost any career or job they want. They can decide to enter politics if they like. And they are free from the close monitoring that so constrained their grandmothers' sexual expression.

Do they understand that it took the energy of thousands of women, during more than a century, to create the society we live in today? They ought to know that feminism is the political movement that has generated the most profound and momentous changes in our society. They should know that feminism created these changes without spilling a single drop of blood. They should realize that

they are the chosen audience of anti-feminists who proclaim that feminism is unnecessary today and that it "harms" women by branding them as victims. Some believe they are assertive enough and don't need to be "feminists." That word sometimes seems so unattractive.

Young women of the 21st century are on the move. They're succeeding at school, college, and university. Will they be able to transform their academic success into equality with men in all areas of their lives?

Hopefully they know that feminism is not something to be dreaded. For over a century, it has fulfilled three essential functions. First, the feminist movement developed a long list of demands that enabled women to gradually take their rightful place in society as citizens, workers, and independent persons with freedom over their sexuality. Secondly, feminists were responsible for setting up social services for women in different eras: Gouttes de lait and Assistance maternelle in the early 20th century, and women's centres and women's shelters since the 1970s. Lastly, thanks to feminism, the consciousness of all women has been raised. And raising women's consciousness is indispensable to changing the world for the better.

The aim of this book has been to convince these young women of the legitimacy of our struggle and its necessity now in the 21th century.

— MICHELINE DUMONT, *July 2012*

Sources of Quotations

All the quotations in the book were translated from the original French. The references for most quotations have been abbreviated. Readers can refer to the Bibliography for the complete reference.

PART ONE

CHAPTER 2
"raise the intellectual level..." Marchand, p. 161; "Its organizers are set on..." Sicotte, p. 136; "Religious questions..." Marchand, note 136, p. 263; "This iron grip will give way..." *ibid.*, p. 164; "As you like..." *ibid.*, p. 166; "What a woman!..." Sicotte, p. 114.

CHAPTER 3
"This discovery..." Pinard, p. 196; "They are horrible..." Sicotte, p. 118; "These days, it is not well looked upon..." Dumont and Toupin, p. 137; "It seems that what we needed..." *ibid.*, p. 51; "The ice is broken..." Sicotte, p. 185; "to celebrate a French defeat..." Robert Rumilly, *Histoire de la société Saint-Jean-Baptiste de Montréal, des Patriotes au Fleurdelisé.* Montréal, L'Aurore, 1975, p. 198.

CHAPTER 4
"Our association of society matrons..." Béique, p. 227; "since the Fédération..." Dumont and Toupin, p. 27; "I have no choice but to give..." Sicotte, p. 211; "Women's social welfare activities..." *ibid.*; "The secular group..." M. Dumont, "Avelyne Bengle" *Dictionnaire biographique que du Canada* (à paraître); "If you want..." cited in Danylewycz, p. 190.

CHAPTER 5
"The cruel and heartbreaking truth..." Baillargeon, p. 71; "A principle... " Sicotte, p. 236; "In certain circles..." *ibid.*, p. 241.

PART TWO

CHAPTER 6
"They have reinstituted…" Cleverdon, p. 223; "Those who fear…" Jean Letendre, *Les Cercles de fermières 1915-1930. Un exemple d'encadrement politique d'un mouvement populaire féminin*, Université de Sherbrooke, 1983, p. 211.

CHAPTER 7
"We demand…" Dumont and Toupin, p. 163; "The partial vote…" *La Bonne Parole*, September 1917, p. 1.

CHAPTER 8
"Is it the right time…" Sicotte, p. 342-343; "that feminism is a perverse movement…" cited in Jean, p. 47-48; "But you don't have to answer…" Sicotte, p. 360.

CHAPTER 9
"As destructive as the horrors…" Sicotte, p. 375; "The women's vote…" *ibid.*, p. 411; "If we give women the vote…" Dumont and Toupin, p. 185; "Feminism is a disease…" *Le Devoir*, 5 April 1928; "Woman must desert…" *ibid.*

CHAPTER 10
"I may be a feminist…" Dumont and Toupin, p. 178; "Man will abolish…" Jean, p. 74; "Québec is the laughing-stock…" Dumont and Toupin, p. 41; "The injury…" Clio Collective, p. 359.

CHAPTER 11
"women who are worn out…" Halpern, p. 36; "Nurses do not…" cited in Johanne Daigle, "L'éveil syndical des 'religieuses laïques': l'émergence et l'évolution de l'Alliance des infirmières de Montréal," in Lavigne and Pinard, p. 120; "Prayers don't build…" in a television interview; "A female labourer…" Dumont and Toupin, p. 110; "These government men…" *ibid.*, p. 111; "I respect my husband's ideas…" *Histoire du mouvement des femmes au Saguenay-Lac-Saint-Jean*, Jonquière, La Chambarde, p. 91; "A good-hearted woman…" Dumont, 1981, p. 20.

CHAPTER 12
"We are not in favour…" Clio Collective, p. 265; "Our real work…" Dumont and Toupin, p. 221.

PART THREE

CHAPTER 13
"Ménagères…" Auger and Lamothe, p. 60; "De la poêle à frire…" *ibid.*, flyleaf; "Governing means planning ahead" Dumont and Toupin, p. 123.

CHAPTER 14

"Since women have been favoured with the right to vote..." Léon Lebel, *L'État et les associations professionnelles* (1944 brochure), p. 13; "Madam, if this is your view..." Auger and Lamothe, p. 104; "So that's how it is. Women in the rest of the country have it given to them ..." *ibid.*, p. 104; "*The Civil Code* is an incomparable monument..." Dumont and Toupin, p. 329.

CHAPTER 15

"If they were unequal, women had only themselves to blame" Dumont and Toupin, p. 432; "We don't have to ask ourselves..." *ibid.*, p. 281; "It is unjust to prevent a woman..." *ibid.*; "If we do not want young women to work..." *ibid.*, p. 117; the eight quotations at the end of the chapter are from the special insert in *Le Devoir*, 23 June 1961.

CHAPTER 16

"Any committee composed solely of women..." Paré, p. 54; "Are women going to have to do it ourselves?" Réjane Laberge-Colas, "L'incapacité de la femme mariée," *La revue du Barreau*, vol. 13, 10 December 1963; "if we are consistent with our own principles" Dumont and Toupin, p. 400; "Women unite!" *ibid.*, p. 438; "My goal..." heard on television; "It looks like the major phenomenon..." archives of reporters associated with the Cercle des femmes journalistes.

CHAPTER 17

"Wake up..." Dumont and Toupin, p. 439; "The era of recriminations..." *Le Devoir*, 26 April 1965, p. 3; "A new image..." *La Presse*, 26 April 1965, p. 3; "A new strike force" *La Presse*, 28 April 1965, p. 4; "No," answered the first president" *Bulletin de la FFQ*, March 1976, p. 22; "The predominant theme..." Lamoureux and others, p. 53; "Women's associations..." *Le Devoir*, 4 October 1966; "Feminism and women's groups..." *Le Devoir*, 15 April 1966.

CHAPTER 18

"We do not need to minimize..." Dumont and Toupin, p. 259; "We don't believe..." *Bulletin de la FFQ*, March 1976, p. 8; "If I can become..." Lysiane Gagnon, *Vivre avec les hommes. Un nouveau partage*, Montréal: Québec Amérique, 1983, p. 199; "I want to see global social change first..." O'Leary and Toupin, Vol. 1, p. 201.

PART FOUR

CHAPTER 19

"Feminism? You mean..." L. Gagnon, p. 197; "Le Front commun des Québécoises..." O'Leary and Toupin, Vol. 1, p. 54; "When you say that..." O'Leary and Toupin, Vol. 2, p. 329; "Or they say..." *ibid.*; "I was really angry..." *ibid.*, p. 342; "In the workers committee..." *ibid.*, p. 349; "Feminists are crazy!" Thérèse Casgrain, telephone conversation with a feminist activist in 1971.

CHAPTER 20

"Reine un jour..." O'Leary and Toupin, Vol. 1, p. 72; "We refuse..." *ibid.*, p. 71; "Mariage = prostitution légalisée" *ibid.*, p. 70; "What? Women don't have the right..." Péloquin, p. 36; "Discrimination!" *ibid.*, p. 41; "The justice system..." *ibid.*; "They're raping us..." *ibid.*, p. 42; "We don't want your..." O'Leary and Toupin, Vol. 1, p. 97-98; "Being in the heat of the action..." *Les Têtes de pioche*, p. 115; "Most of the activists..." *ibid.*

CHAPTER 21

"We recommend that the *Criminal Code*..." Report of the Bird Commission, p. 464; "In my view..." *ibid.*, p. 483; "would be concerned with..." *ibid.*, p. 470; "Our brief is..." Committee archives; "The FFQ is a serious..." *Bulletin de la FFQ*, March 1976, p. 15; "You have to be rich..." *Bulletin de la FFQ*, November 1975, p. 3.

CHAPTER 22

"Nous aurons les enfants..." Desmarais, cited throughout; "They [have] ignored rural women..." *La Gazette des femmes*, Vol. 1, No. 1.

CHAPTER 23

"These transition houses..." Lacombe, p. 75.

CHAPTER 24

"Women from the suburbs..." *L'Actualité*, October 1972, p. 40; "We rarely heard women say..." *ibid.*; "My son the judge..." from the film *They Called us Les Filles du Roy*; "I console..." *ibid.*; "So many of us..." *L'Actualité*, October 1972, p. 48; "I'm sorry to..." "La femme et l'écriture," *Liberté*, July-October 1976, p. 34; "It took me a few months..." *ibid.*, p.77; "the act of writing..." Brossard, p. 53; "Reading *L'Euguélionne*..." *Les Têtes de pioche*, p. 135; "Marriage appeared to be..." Yolande Dupuis, "Francine Larivée et *La Chambre nuptiale*," *Sysiphe*, 11 April 2005.

CHAPTER 25

"Feminism is the theory..." slogan of the times; "You heteros" heard in class rooms; "We were supposed..." *Les Têtes de pioche*, p. 156; "This is how..." *ibid.*; "We want independence..." Yanacopoulo, p. 30.

CHAPTER 26

"Speaking for myself..." Godin, p. 50; "Guy likes..." *ibid.*, p. 52; "We must have the courage..." *ibid.*, p. 53; "In fact, he's married..." *ibid.*; "Linking a woman..." *ibid.*; "In insulting Madeleine..." *ibid.*, p. 54; "If my remark..." *ibid.*, p. 55; "It could have a boomerang..." *ibid.*, p. 58; "The péquistes...", *ibid.*, p. 63; "They wanted to make fun..." Caron and others, p. 193; "We had to..." *ibid.*; "We wanted to show them..." *ibid.*; "It was a way..." *ibid.*; "It gave us the courage..." *ibid.*; "For me, it was..." *ibid.*

PART FIVE

CHAPTER 27
"Our real work has just begun..." Dumont and Toupin, p. 222; "If we give women..." *ibid.*, p. 185; "Did you get the special issue on women..." personal experience of author.

CHAPTER 28
"When I mentioned that" *Approches et méthodes de la recherche féministe*, Québec, GREMF, 1986, p. 278; "It was a real shock..." Dumont and Toupin, p. 447; "It's a new trend..." *La Petite Presse*, June 1986, p. 3; "I find it really frustrating..." Radio-Canada, CBFT, 19 August 1980, comments about the 'Yvettes' phenomenon; "Measures must be taken..." Dumont and Toupin, p. 149; "Man needed..." job postings board, Université de Sherbrooke, 1988; "For every woman..." *La Vie en rose*, January 1984, p. 11; "If you do that..." *La Vie en rose*, February 1985, p. 11; "This law divides families..." *Histoire des femmes au Témiscamingue*, Collectif témiscamien, 1988, p. 61; "The bishops in the lion's den!", Montréal parish newsletter.

CHAPTER 29
"A magazine covering current events..." *La Vie en rose*, special issue, 2005, p. 7; "Do we like men?" *La Vie en rose*, June 1982, p. 4; "We went off to tend..." *La Vie en rose*, special issue, 2005, p. 10; "racers in a huge relay race" Godbout, p. 9; "Prends-le pas..." *ibid.*, cited throughout; "You can't make activist art!" Pierre Vadeboncœur, *Trois essais sur l'insignifiance*, Montréal: L'Hexagone, 1983, p. 62.

CHAPTER 30
"They [the feminists] are undeniably right." Georges-Hébert Germain, "Le syndrome du bourdon," *L'Actualité*, April 1984, p. 44; "Men are silent..." *ibid.*; "Feminism has killed romance" *ibid.*; "Feminism has caused..." *ibid.*, p. 46; "Feminism is hypocritical" *ibid.*, p. 47; "It makes sense ..." Dominique Demers, "Féminisme, mission accomplie?" *L'Actualité*, Dec. 1984, p. 124; "Women have no business..." heard on a radio hotline show (CHLT, Sherbrooke, Québec), 8 March 1985; "Women's magazines..." comment heard at the Centre de santé des femmes de Sherbrooke; "Oh! Feminism is so old hat!" heard on Radio-Canada, TV news broadcast on women's magazines; "Today, feminism is much less..." Beauchamp, p. 188; "What do feminists do?" *Châtelaine*, May 1986; "They are cruel and murderous females." Desmarais, p. 283; "The scope of this judgment..." *ibid.*, p. 339; "The foetus is not included..." *ibid.*, p. 350; "You're all just a bunch of feminists!" reported in the media on 7 December 1989; "We're not feminists..." *ibid.*; "Even though the media... *La Vie en rose*, special issue 2005, p. 36; "He should have..." *ibid.*, p. 35; "We know from a very good source..." Godbout, p. 225; "Feminists are trying..." heard in media coverage; "I'm amazed there haven't been more..." Radio-Canada archives, 6 December 1989; "Next to these exaggerated..." Roch Côté, *Manifeste d'un salaud*, Terrebonne: Éd. du Portique, 1990; "I experienced Roch Côté's Manifeste..." Louis Cornellier, "Le féminisme et moi," *Le Devoir*, 1 December 2007.

CHAPTER 31

"To our true mothers..." *Femmes en tête*, p. 12; "After the tragic..." *ibid.*, p. 13; "I decided to accept..." *Gazette des femmes*, Sept.-Oct. 1990. p. 12; "How do you justify..." Roch Côté, *Manifeste d'un salaud*, Terrebonne, Éd. du Portique, 1990; "if there were another..." *La Petite Presse*; "The distinct society clause..." Roberts, p. 6; "In fact, the progress..." *ibid.*, p. 13; "Women were told..." L. Pagé, "Les femmes dans le Québec de demain," *Action nationale*, May 1991, p. 623; "From a feminist point of view..." Maillé, p. 64; "We've broken the ice..." Sicotte, p. 185.

CHAPTER 32

"The word feminism..." Guindon, p. 60; "That was a movement..." *ibid.*, p. 64; "Maybe we would be..." *ibid.*, p. 76; "If I had to choose..." *ibid.*, p. 89; "A wind of change..." *ibid.*, p. 29; "It's not a march..." video by Paula McKeown, *Désirs de liberté*.

CHAPTER 33

"The values [in the Charter]..." document accompanying the *Women's World Charter for Humanity*.

CHAPTER 34

"Shouldn't women..." Breton, p. 122; "I think the way girls are acting..." *Châtelaine*, October 2000, p. 94; "The hypersexualization..." *Gazette des femmes*, September-October 2005, p. 19; "It took some consciousness-raising..." *La Tribune*, 22 February 2008, p. S3; "Women's bodies..." Breton, p. 113.

Bibliography

Except for the first four works, which are more general in scope, the bibliography has been grouped according to the book's five parts. In this way, readers can consult all the references for a particular period of feminism in Québec.

Caron, Anita, ed. *Thérèse Casgrain. Une femme tenace et engagée*. Montréal: Presses de l'Université du Québec, 1993.

Clio Collective. *Quebec Women: A History*. Originally published in French as *Histoire des femmes au Québec depuis quatre siècles*. Translated by Roger Gannon and Rosalind Gill. Toronto: The Women's Press, 1987.

Dumont, Micheline and Louise Toupin. *La pensée féministe au Québec: Anthologie 1900-1985*. Montréal: Remue-ménage, 2003.

Jean, Michèle. *Québécoises du xxe siècle*. Montréal: Éd. du Jour, 1974.

PART 1: WOMEN ORGANIZE

Baillargeon, Denyse. *Un Québec en mal d'enfants. La médicalisation de la maternité, 1910-1970*. Montréal: Remue-ménage, 2004.

Béique, Caroline. *Quatre-vingts ans de souvenirs. Histoire d'une famille*. Montréal: Valiquette, 1939.

Danylewycz, Marta. *Profession: religieuse. Un choix pour les Québécoises, 1840-1920*. Montréal: Boréal, 1988.

Dumont, Micheline. "L'accès à l'instruction et à la mixité," in F. Thébaud and others, eds., *Le siècle des féminismes*. Paris: L'Atelier, 2004, p. 149-162.

Fahmy-Eid, Nadia. "La presse féminine au Québec, 1890-1920: une pratique politique et culturelle ambivalente," in Y. Cohen, ed., *Femmes et politique*. Montréal: Éd. du Jour, 1981, p. 101-115.

Fahmy-Eid, Nadia and Micheline Dumont. "Recettes pour la femme idéale: Femmes/famille et éducation dans deux journaux libéraux: Le Canada et La Patrie (1900-1920)," in *Atlantis*, Vol. 10, No. 1, Fall 1984, p. 46-59.

Lavigne, Marie, Yolande Pinard and Jennifer Stoddart. "La Fédération nationale Saint-Jean-Baptiste et les revendications féministes au début du 20e siècle," in M. Lavigne and Y. Pinard, eds., *Travailleuses et féministes: Les femmes dans la société québécoise*. Montréal: Boréal, 1983, p. 199-216.

Marchand Joséphine. *Journal intime, 1879-1900*. Montréal: La pleine lune, 2000.

Pinard, Yolande. "Les débuts du mouvement des femmes à Montréal, 1893-1902," in M. Lavigne and Y. Pinard eds., *Travailleuses et féministes: Les femmes dans la société québécoise*. Montréal: Boréal, 1983, p. 177-198.

Sicotte, Anne-Marie. *Marie Gérin-Lajoie, conquérante de la liberté*. Montréal: Remue-ménage, 2005.

Strong-Boag, Veronica. *The Parliament of Women: The National Council of Women of Canada, 1893-1923*. Ottawa: Musées nationaux du Canada, 1976.

PART 2: FEMINISTS CAMPAIGN FOR WOMEN'S VOTING RIGHTS

La Bonne Parole, magazine of the Fédération nationale Saint-Jean-Baptiste.

Cleverdon, Catherine L. *The Woman Suffrage Movement in Canada*. Toronto: University of Toronto Press, 1974.

Darsigny, Maryse. *L'épopée du suffrage féminin au Québec (1920-1940)*. Montréal: UQAM/Relais-femmes, 1990.

La femme canadienne-française. Montréal: Almanach de la langue française, 1936.

Halpern, Sylvie. *Le Chaînon: la maison de Montréal*. Montréal: Stanké, 1998.

Jean, Michèle. "Idola Saint-Jean, féministe (1880-1945)," in *Mon héroïne*. Montréal: Remue-ménage, 1981, p. 117-148.

Lamoureux, Diane. *Citoyennes? Femmes, droit de vote et démocratie*. Montréal: Remue-ménage, 1989.

Lavigne, Marie, Yolande Pinard and Jennifer Stoddart. "La Fédération nationale Saint-Jean-Baptiste et les revendications féministes au début du 20e siècle," in M. Lavigne and Y. Pinard, eds., *Travailleuses et féministes: Les femmes dans la société québécoise*. Montréal: Boréal, 1983, p. 199-216.

Sicotte, Anne-Marie. *Marie Gérin-Lajoie, conquérante de la liberté*. Montréal: Remue-ménage, 2005.

Trifiro, Luigi. "Une intervention à Rome en 1922 dans la lutte pour le suffrage féminin," *Revue d'histoire de l'Amérique française*, Vol. 32, No. 1, June 1978, p. 3-18.

PART 3: NOW FULL-FLEDGED CITIZENS, WOMEN SEEK TO TAKE THEIR PLACE IN SOCIETY

Auger, Geneviève and Raymonde Lamothe. *De la poêle à frire à la ligne de feu: La vie quotidienne des Québécoises pendant la guerre 39-45*. Montréal: Boréal, 1981.

Le Devoir, special issue, 23 June 1961.

Dumont, Micheline. "La parole des femmes: Les revues féminines, 1938-1968," in *Idéologies au Canada français, 1940-1976*, Vol. II: *Les mouvements sociaux*. F. Dumont, ed. Québec City: Presses de l'Université Laval, 1981, p. 5-46.

Dumont, Micheline. "Historienne et sujet de l'histoire," *Questions de culture*, No. 8. Québec City: Institut québécois de recherche sur la culture, 1986, p. 21-34.

Dumont, Micheline. "The Origins of the Women's Movement in Quebec," in *Challenging Times: The Contemporary Women's Movement in Canada and the United States*. D.H. Flaherty and C. Backhouse, eds. Montréal: McGill-Queen's University Press, 1992, p. 72-89.

Gosselin, Cheryl A. *Vers l'avenir. Quebec Women's Politics Between 1945 and 1967: Feminist, Maternalist and Nationalist Links*. Doctoral dissertation (history), Université de Montréal, 2002.

McKeown, Paula. *Désirs de liberté*. Video produced by the CEQ, l'Intersyndicale des femmes and Vidéo-femmes, 1995.

Paré, Hélène. *Les comités de condition féminine dans les syndicats*. Montréal: Secretary of State, Status of Women Program, Québec Region, 1983.

Report of the Royal Commission on the Status of Women in Canada. Ottawa, 1970.

Rialland-Morissette, Yvonne. *Le passé conjugué au présent, Cercles de fermières du Québec: Historique, 1915-1980*. Montréal: Pénélope, 1980.

PART 4: THE GREAT FEMINIST STIRRING

Boucher, Denise. *Les fées ont soif.* Montréal: Intermède, 1978.

Brossard, Nicole. *L'amèr ou Le chapitre effrité.* Montréal: L'Hexagone, coll. Typo, 1988.

Bulletin de la Fédération des femmes du Québec, complete collection.

Couillard, Danielle. *Féminisme et nationalisme. Histoire d'une ambiguïté: L'expérience du Regroupement des femmes québécoises.* Master's thesis (history), Université de Montréal, 1987.

Desmarais, Louise. *Mémoires d'une bataille inachevée: La lutte pour l'avortement au Québec.* Montréal: Trait d'union, 1999.

Dumont, Micheline. "Le mouvement des femmes à Sherbrooke." *Possibles*, Vol. 18, No. 4. Fall 1994, p. 51-63.

La femme et l'écriture, special issue of *Liberté*, Vol. 18, Nos. 4-5, 1976.

Gagnon, Lysiane. *Vivre avec les hommes. Un nouveau partage.* Montréal: Québec Amérique, 1983.

Godin, Stéphanie. *Les Yvettes comme l'expression d'un féminisme fédéraliste au Québec.* Master's thesis (history), Université du Québec à Montréal, 2003.

Halpern, Sylvie. *Le Chaînon: la maison de Montréal.* Montréal: Stanké, 1998.

Lacombe, Madeleine. *Au grand jour.* Montréal: Remue-ménage, 1990.

Lamoureux, Jocelyne, Michèle Gélinas and Katy Tari. *Femmes en mouvement: Trajectoires de l'Association féminine d'éducation et d'action sociale. AFÉAS, 1966-1991.* Montréal: Boréal, 1993.

Péloquin, Marjolaine. *En prison pour la cause des femmes: La conquête du banc des jurés.* Montréal: Remue-ménage, 2007.

O'Leary, Véronique and Louise Toupin. *Québécoises deboutte!,* Vol. 1, *Une anthologie de textes du Front de libération des femmes (1969-1971) et du Centre des femmes (1972-1975).* Montréal: Remue-ménage, 1982.

O'Leary, Véronique and Louise Toupin. *Québécoises deboutte!,* Vol. 2, *Collection complète des journaux (1972-1974).* Montréal: Remue-ménage, 1983.

Les Têtes de pioche. Journal des femmes. Complete collection. Montréal: Remue-ménage, 1980.

Yanacopoulo, Andrée. *Le Regroupement des femmes québécoises, 1976-1981.* Montréal: Point de fuite/Remue-ménage, 2003.

PART 5: CHANGING THE WORLD

Beauchamp, Colette. *Le silence des medias*. Montréal: Remue-ménage, 1987.

Beauchamp, Colette, Rosette Côté and Sylvie Paquerot, eds. *Pour changer le monde: le forum Pour un Québec féminin pluriel*. Montréal: Écosociété, 1994.

Breton, Émilie and others. "Mon/notre/leur corps est toujours un champ de bataille. Discours féministes et queers libertaires au Québec, 2000-2007." *Recherches féministes*, Vol. 20, No. 2, 2007, p. 113-140.

Collard, Nathalie and Pascale Navarro. *Interdit aux femmes: Le féminisme et la censure de la pornographie*. Montréal: Boréal, 1996.

Desmarais, Louise. *Mémoires d'une bataille inachevée: La lutte pour l'avortement au Québec*. Montréal: Trait d'union, 1999.

Dumont, Micheline. *Le mouvement des femmes, hier et aujourd'hui*. Ottawa: ICREE/CRIAW, comp. Perspectives féministes, No. 5-A, 1986.

Dumont, Micheline. "Réflexions féministes face au pouvoir." In *Mémoires d'un forum de femmes: Des outils pour agir ensemble*. Montréal: CEQ, 1987, p. 15-21.

Dumont, Micheline. "Quebec Women and the Contemporary Constitutional Issue." In *Gender and Politics in Contemporary Canada*. F. P. Gingras, ed. Montréal: McGill-Queen's University Press, 1995, p. 153-173.

Dumont, Micheline and Stéphanie Lanthier. "Pas d'histoire, les femmes. Le féminisme dans un magazine québécois à grand tirage: *L'Actualité*." *Recherches féministes: Ils changent... disent-ils*, Vol. 11, No. 2, 1998, p. 101-124.

Dumont, Micheline. "Réfléchir sur le féminisme du troisième millénaire." In *Dialogues sur la troisième vague féministe*. M. N. Mensah, ed. Montréal: Remue-ménage, 2005, p. 59-73.

Femmes en Tête. *De travail et d'espoir: Des groupes de femmes racontent le féminisme*. Montréal: Remue-ménage, 1990.

La Gazette des femmes. Complete collection, especially the March 1994 issue: Si la tendance se maintient.

Godbout, Lucie. *Les dessous des Folles Alliées: Un livre affriolant*. Montréal: Remue-ménage, 1993.

Guindon, Geneviève. *Les opinions et les perceptions des jeunes femmes à l'égard du féminisme*. Master's thesis (sociology), Université de Montréal, 1996.

Lacelle, Nicole. *À l'école du pouvoir*. Montréal: Remue-ménage, 1999.

Maillé, Chantal. *Cherchez la femme: Trente ans de débats constitutionnels au Québec*. Montréal: Remue-ménage, 2002.

Malette, Louise and Marie Chalouh, eds. *Polytechnique, 6 décembre*. Montréal: Remue-ménage, 1990.

La Petite Presse, journal of the Fédération des femmes du Québec. Complete collection.

Quéniart, Anne and Julie Jacques. *Apolitiques, les jeunes femmes?* Montréal: Remue-ménage, 2004.

Roberts, Barbara. *Beau fixe ou nuage à l'horizon: L'Accord du lac Meech jugé par les groupes féministes du Québec et du Canada*. Ottawa: ICREF/CRIAW, comp. Perspectives féministes, No. 12.

Toupin, Louise. "Analyser autrement la 'prostitution' et la 'traite des femmes.'" *Recherches féministes*, Vol. 19, No. 1, 2006, p. 153-176.

Toupin, Louise. "La scission politique du féminisme international sur la question du 'trafic des femmes': vers la 'migration' d'un certain féminisme radical." *Recherches féministes*, Vol. 15, No. 2, 2002, p. 9-40.

Verdière, Brigitte. *Women on the March: Focus on the Actions and Demands of the World March of Women*. Montréal: Marche mondiale des femmes/Remue-ménage, 2002.

La Vie en rose. Complete collection (1980-1987) and special issue. Montréal: Remue-ménage, 2005.

Photo Credits

Thank you to Emelie Kozak and Jessica Kozak, who undertook the photo research for this book with thoughtfulness, diligence and organization.

Every effort has been made to trace the original source of photographs in this book. Where the attempt has been unsuccessful, we would be pleased to hear from copyright holders so that we can rectify any omission in subsequent editions.

DUSTJACKET Bibliothèque et Archives nationales du Québec, Direction du Centre d'archives de Montréal / Fonds Conrad Poirier / P48, S1, P7079 / Girl at Gas Station Joy (August 1, 1941)

PAGE 8: Courtesy of Micheline Dumont

PAGES 10 & 11: Bibliothèque et Archives nationales du Québec, Direction du Centre d'archives de Montréal / Collection Institut Notre-Dame du Bon-Conseil de Montréal / P783, S2, SS9

PAGE 17: Library and Archives Canada / PA-027856/ Topley Studio

PAGE 18: Bibliothèque et Archives nationales du Québec / Tirée de *Le Monde illustré*, vol. 1, no.4, p. 25, 31 mai 1884.

PAGE 20: Courtesy of the Éditions de la Pleine Lune

PAGE 21: Library and Archives Canada / PA-212948 / Harold Mortimer-Lamb

PAGE 24: Bibliothèque et Archives nationales du Québec / National Council of Women

PAGE 25: Library and Archives Canada / PA-028033 / Topley Studio

PAGE 26: Library and Archives Canada / NLC-8133

PAGE 29: Bibliothèque et Archives nationales du Québec, Direction du Centre d'archives de Montréal / Collection Institut Notre-Dame du Bon-Conseil de Montréal / P783, S2, SS9, P2 / U.2.2

PAGE 30: Bibliothèque et Archives nationales du Québec, Direction du Centre d'archives de Montréal / Collection Institut Notre-Dame du Bon-Conseil de Montréal / P783, S2, SS9

PAGE 35: Archives du CHU Sainte-Justine

PAGES 40 & 41: Bibliothèque et Archives nationales du Québec, Direction du Centre d'archives de Montréal / Collection initiale / P318, S2, P56

PAGE 43: Library and Archives Canada / C-068506 / Catherine Lyle Cleverdon / William Notman & Son

PAGE 51: Bibliothèque et Archives nationales du Québec / Série Revues anciennes / no 2688, séquence 2747242

PAGE 52: Library and Archives Canada / PA-127291 / Dupras & Colas

PAGE 54: Bibliothèque et Archives nationales du Québec, Direction du Centre d'archives de Montréal / Collection initiale / P318, S2, P56

PAGE 61: *La Patrie*, 10 février 1922

PAGE 63: Courtesy of the Léa Roback Foundation

PAGE 64: Bibliothèque et Archives nationales du Québec, Direction du Centre d'archives de Montréal / Collection Institut Notre-Dame du Bon-Conseil de Montréal / P783, S2, SS9, P2 / E.10

PAGE 69: Archives *La Presse* / 11717709 / Conseil de la Ligue pour les Droits de la Femme

PAGE 72: Bibliothèque et Archives nationales du Québec, Direction du Centre d'archives de Montréal / Fonds Conrad Poirier / P48, S1, P7079 / Girl at Gas Station Joy (August 1, 1941)

PAGES 74 & 75: Bibliothèque et Archives nationales du Québec, Direction du Centre d'archives de Montréal / Fonds Conrad Poirier / P48, S1, P9128

PAGE 77: Source unknown

PAGE 78: Source unknown

PAGE 81: Library and Archives Canada / PA-178177 / Yousuf Karsh

PAGE 87: Courtesy of l'Université de Montréal

PAGE 93: Library and Archives Canada / C-051887 / Arthur Roy

PAGE 94: Courtesy of the Chartrand Family

PAGE 95: Bibliothèque et Archives nationales du Québec, Centre d'archives de Montréal / Fonds du Ministère de la Culture et des Communications / E6, S7, SS1, D710131

PAGE 100: Courtesy of John Reeves

PAGE 101: Archives of the Fédération des femmes du Québec

PAGE 102: Archives of the Association féminine d'éducation et d'action sociale (AFÉAS)

PAGE 105: Courtesy of Harry Palmer

PAGE 106: Library and Archives Canada / E002415954 / Status of Women Canada

PAGES 110 & 111: Archives of the Fédération du Québec pour le planning des naissances

PAGE 116: Archives and Special Collections, University of Ottawa Library / (X10-93) / Montreal Health Press

PAGE 117: O'Leary, Véronique et Toupin, Louise (ed.) *Québécoises Deboutte!*, Tome 1, *Une anthologie de textes du Front de libération des femmes (1969-1971) et du Centre des femmes (1972-1975)*, Montréal, les éditions du remue-ménage, 1982, p. 72

PAGE 119: *Québécoises deboutte!*, Vol. 1, No. 1, November 1971

PAGE 124: Archives of the Fédération des femmes du Québec

PAGE 127: Courtesy of John Reeves

PAGE 130: Archives of the Fédération du Québec pour le planning des naissances

PAGE 132: Archives of the Association féminine d'éducation et d'action sociale (AFÉAS)

Page 137: Courtesy of John Reeves

Page 138: Service des bibliothèques et archives de l'Université de Sherbrooke / Théâtre du Nouveau Monde, Fonds André Le Coz / P29 / M105

PAGE 141: Courtesy of Kèro Beaudoin

PAGE 142: Courtesy of Francine Larivée / produced in collaboration with the Groupe de recherche et d'action sociale par l'art et les médias (GRASAM) / photo by Marc Cramer

PAGE 149 Left: Fédération des femmes du Québec, *La Petite Presse*, Vol. 5, No. 5, March 1986

PAGE 149 Right: *Les Têtes de pioche*, Vol. 2, No. 3, May 1977

PAGE 150: *L'Autre Parole*, No. 1, 1976; *Pluri-elles*, newsletter of independent women's groups, Vol. 1, No. 6, June 1978; *Des luttes et des rires de femmes*, newsletter of independent women's groups, Vol. 2, No. 1, Oct. / Nov. 1978; *Communiqu'Elles*, Vol. 16, No. 5, September 1989

PAGE 151: Conseil du statut de la femme

PAGE 152: Conseil du statut de la femme

PAGE 154: Bibliothèque et Archives nationales du Québec / Centre d'archives et des communications / E6, S7, SS1, D8005923

PAGE 156: *La Tribune* / April 22, 1980, page A1

PAGES 162 & 163: Courtesy of Lucie Godbout / Michel Lemay

PAGE 166: Conseil du statut de la femme

PAGE 172: Front commun intersyndical (CSN-FTQ-CEQ) for IWD, 8 March 1982 / Graveline and Champagne

PAGE 178: Courtesy of *La Vie en rose* collective

PAGE 179: Courtesy of Lucie Godbout / Michel Lemay

PAGE 180: Courtesy of Lucie Godbout / Jacques Girard

PAGE 185: *La Presse* / Jean Goupil / 852811

PAGE 191: Archives of the Fédération des femmes du Québec

PAGE 199: Courtesy of Françoise David

PAGE 200: Archives of the Fédération des femmes du Québec

PAGE 205: Archives of the Fédération des femmes du Québec

PAGE 206: Archives of the Fédération des femmes du Québec

PAGE 208: Archives of the Fédération des femmes du Québec

PAGE 211: Courtesy of Robert Etcheverry

PAGE 212: Archives of Stella

PAGE 219: Private Collection

Acknowledgements

THE PEOPLE I WISH TO THANK are so numerous that I'm certain to forget someone, and for this, I apologize. There were too many papers on my desk, too many names scribbled in my address book, too many to-do lists around the computer.

My editors, of course, Élise Bergeron and Rachel Bédard of les Éditions du remue-ménage, for their infinite patience and professional, painstaking and intelligent work. Also Erika Fixot, an intern who handled the complicated task of the illustrations with such panache. They had faith in me and even announced my book's arrival while I was still labouring to organize a huge mountain of material and almost losing my way in the process! And, of course—just look at my bibliography—what would I have done without the dozens of books les Éditions du remue-ménage have published over the years!

For this English translation, I thank the Feminist History Society/Société d'histoire féministe, especially Constance Backhouse and Beth Symes, for their dedication in seeing the project through; Nicole Kennedy, able translator, for capturing the simplicity of the original prose; and Sarah Swartz, for editing the English manuscript.

I thank my readers: Camille Johnson, high school student, Frédérique Blache-Pichette, CÉGEP student, Valérie Dubé, university student, and Stéphanie Lanthier (in her 30's), Nicole Charrette (in her 50's) and Suzanne Dumont (in her 60's). The younger women listed all the words they weren't familiar with. Feminist activists pointed out my omissions and contradictions; they discussed my interpretations of events, helped me to refine my thinking and compared their memories with my own.

My sincere appreciation to the women who provided me with information, dates, names, explanations, interpretations and references and those who loaned me their archives, photographs, articles, journals, books and course notes and referred me to websites: Denyse Baillargeon, Monique Bégin, Maude Benny-Dumont, Colette Bernier, Sister Florence Bertrand, Isabelle Boisclair, Pierrette Bouchard, Nicole Boudreau, Nancy Burrows, Ginette Busque, Renée B. Dandurand, Solange Cantin, Lyne Chamberland, Laurette Champigny-Robillard, Nicole Charrette, Renée Cloutier, Johanne Daigle, Maria De Koninck, Lise Drouin-Paquette, Nicole Dorin, Lise Gratton, Marie Gratton, Sharon Gray, Kèro, Anna Kruzynski, Francine Larivée, Andrée Lévesque, Stéphanie McKibbin, Odette Michaud, Hélène Pednault, Marjolaine Péloquin, Christine Piette, Louise Riendeau, France Rioux, Évelyne Tardy, Louise Toupin, Flavie Trudel and Sister Gisèle Turcot.

And, of course, I thank my family, especially Rodrigue, for calming me down when I was raging against my computer or desperately hunting a misplaced book, and sustaining and pampering me with his tasty dishes. Over three years went by between the first draft and publication, and that's a lot of dishes!